BLAST OFF!

on

New Jersey Reading

ESPA Book 4

Buckle Down
PUBLISHING COMPANY

Acknowledgments

Excerpt from JENNIFER MURDLEY'S TOAD. Copyright © 1992 by Bruce Coville.
Reprinted by permission of Harcourt Brace & Company.

Every effort has been made by the publisher to locate each owner of the copyrighted material reprinted
in this publication and to secure the necessary permissions. If there are any questions regarding the use
of these materials, the publisher will take appropriate corrective measures to acknowledge ownership in
future publications.

TABLE OF CONTENTS

Introduction

Think of something you do well. Maybe you are good at kicking a soccer ball, playing the piano, or playing your favorite video game. Everyone has something they're good at. What's your "thing"?

Now think back to the time you first tried the thing you do so well. Were you good at it from the very start? Or were you a little klutzy, sending the ball out-of-bounds or hitting all the wrong notes?

Whatever your special skill, you can probably remember a time when you weren't as good as you are now. Maybe it seemed hard at first, and you started slowly. But with practice, you got better and better. Perhaps someone helped you—a coach, a teacher, a best friend. They told you the things you did well and pointed out ways you could improve. And look at you now!

Show off your reading skills

Remember when you first learned to read? You knew only a few words in the beginning. But the more you worked at it, the better you got. Now here you are in the fourth grade, reading all kinds of things.

This year you will take a state reading test. The test will help you and your teachers know how you are doing in basic reading skills. It will show what you do well and how you can improve.

Blast Off on New Jersey Reading will help you get ready for the state reading test. We'll show you what to expect. The passages and questions in this book are similar to the kinds you'll see on the test. We'll also give you several tips for answering the different question types. By the time you finish, you'll think of the state test as a way to show off your reading skills.

Ready?

A Reader Training Program

Great athletes don't just wake up one morning and decide to run a marathon. They follow training programs to help them improve on their natural abilities.

You can have a training program for reading, too. Think about it: What's the most important part of training to be a runner? Running, of course. If an athlete wants to be a good runner, he or she has to run—a lot. If you want to be a good reader, you have to read—a lot. It doesn't matter so much what you read, just that you read a little bit every day.

This doesn't mean you always have to read books. Reading material is everywhere. The list below gives a few ideas for places to look. Add your own ideas as you think of them, or ask your classmates to share their ideas.

✍

- ❏ fast-food menus
- ❏ cereal boxes
- ❏ the back of a toothpaste tube
- ❏ billboards
- ❏ movie reviews
- ❏ yellow page ads for skateboards, bicycles, or whatever interests you
- ❏ a recipe for your favorite kind of cookie or cake (You might even want to bake it for your family.)
- ❏ a newspaper article about your favorite sports team

✍

- ❏ the comic strips in your local newspaper
- ❏ all the fortunes in a package of fortune cookies
- ❏ the jokes in a copy of *Reader's Digest*
- ❏ _____
- ❏ _____
- ❏ _____
- ❏ _____
- ❏ _____

Your Training Log

Athletes often keep a training log. A training log is a type of journal used to record the things you do in your training program. A page in your training log might look something like this.

BOOKS I HAVE READ
The Werewolf of Fever Swamp by R. L. Stine
Shh! We're Writing the Constitution by Jean Fritz
My Name is María Isabel by Alma Flor Ada

BOOKS I WANT TO READ
Tales of a Fourth Grade Nothing by Judy Blume
Mop, Moondance, and the Nagasaka Knights
    by Walter Dean Myers
Hurricanes by Patricia Lauber

OTHER THINGS I WANT TO READ ABOUT
in-line skating
sharks
Native American legends

You may wish to write longer entries about the books you especially liked. You might tell why you liked the book, what you didn't like, feelings or ideas you had while reading, questions that came into your mind, or new words you learned.

To create your own training log, all you need is a spiral-bound notebook and a sprinkling of imagination. Decorate the cover of your log with drawings, paintings, comic strips, or a collage—something to make it uniquely yours. Then keep your training log with you to jot down your reading ideas.

What's on the test?

The test you will take is called the New Jersey Elementary School Proficiency Assessment, or ESPA for short. It will include poetry, made-up stories (**fiction**), and articles about real people, places, things, and events (**nonfiction**). Some of the passages will be interesting. Some may make you want to snooze.

After reading each passage, you'll answer several questions about what you read. This book will give tips and practice in answering the types of questions on the test. If you work carefully through each lesson, you'll know exactly what to expect on test day.

General Tips for Taking the ESPA

 Pay attention to the directions.

Read all the directions in your test book, and listen carefully to the directions your teacher reads to you. If you do not understand some of the directions, ask your teacher to explain them.

 Read every word of the passage.

Read the entire passage before looking at the questions. Don't skip over anything. Reading every word will help you find out what the passage is *mainly* about. And it will help you remember where to find answers to the questions.

If you need to, you may slow down or go back over a difficult idea. But don't get stuck. Keep moving until you come to the end of the passage.

 Read each question carefully.

Read each question and each answer choice slowly and carefully. Don't jump ahead and select an answer before you've read the entire question and *all* the answer choices.

Tip 4 **Use information from the passage to choose your answer.**

You're being tested on your reading skills, not on how much you know about the topic of the passage. Always base your answer on information given in the passage. You may look back at the passage as often as you need to.

Tip 5 **Use key words to find the answer.**

Key words in the questions often point to where the answer can be found in the passage. By learning to identify key words, you'll improve your ability to answer questions quickly and correctly. Key words will be discussed in detail later in this book.

Tip 6 **Don't let hard questions freak you out.**

Some questions might be easy to answer. Others might seem more difficult. If you come to a difficult question, don't panic. Think carefully about what the question is asking. If it seems too difficult, skip it and go on to answer the other questions about the passage. Then, before going on to the next passage, come back to the question you skipped. Try to answer it. If you still don't know the answer, take a guess.

Tip 7 **Answer every question, even if you have to guess.**

If you don't know an answer on the test, give it your best guess. Cross out the answers you know are wrong and pick from the ones that are left. If you don't answer a question, you can't possibly get it right.

Tip 8 **Relax and have fun!**

Just like a runner training for a race, you are "in training" for the state reading test. When test day rolls around, you'll be ready—"in shape"—for the test. And because you'll be ready, you can relax and have fun with it.

On your mark, get set, *go!*

Reading the Lines

Lesson 1

The Big Picture

The **main idea** of a reading passage tells what the passage is *mostly* about. Sometimes the author puts the main idea in a sentence. Sometimes you have to figure it out on your own.

Read the paragraph below from *About Animals,* a Childcraft book.

> You can always tell a turtle by its shell. A box turtle has a high, round shell that it can close up like a box. A map turtle has a wide, flat shell with bumpy edges. A soft-shelled turtle's shell looks like a green pancake.

1. Which sentence from the paragraph tells what the paragraph is *mostly* about?

_____

_____

_____

Sometimes the main idea isn't stated in a sentence. You have to read the passage and figure out the main idea on your own.

Read the following paragraph from *A Cricket in Times Square* by George Selden. Then write a sentence that tells the main idea.

> "Catch the mouse!" shouted Mama. She picked up a *Fortune* magazine—very big and heavy—and heaved it after Tucker. It hit him on the left hind leg just as he vanished into the drain pipe.

2. What is the main idea of the paragraph?

_____

_____

_____

Main Idea Tips

Here are a few tips to help you find the main idea of a reading passage.

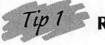 **Read the entire passage first.**

Before you can find the main idea of a passage, you must read the whole passage.

 Decide whether the passage is fiction or nonfiction.

Nonfiction passages are about real things. **Fiction** passages are about made-up things. Many nonfiction passages, like the paragraph on turtles, will tell you the main idea in a sentence. Most fiction passages, like the paragraph from *A Cricket in Times Square*, will not. If you want to know the main idea of a fiction passage, you almost always have to figure it out on your own.

Practice Passage

Directions: Read the story "Getting to Know Gramps." It will help you understand the lesson.

Getting to Know Gramps

by Peter S. Douglas

When I was ten, my grandfather came to live with us. I'd never even seen him before; he was a stranger to me. Mom said that for twenty-five years he'd been the foreman on a cattle ranch in California. When Gramps showed up, I was surprised. He seemed too young to be eighty. He walked easily without a cane, though he did have a walking stick.

Just about all Gramps did that first week was whittle his stick. He sat on the back porch wearing a cowboy hat that looked too big for him. He took a knife out of his pocket and began to carve at the stick's handle. He silently whittled away the hours while a pile of curled wood chips grew beside him.

One day after I got home from school, I found him rubbing his walking stick with a piece of fine sandpaper. "How's it going, Gramps?" I asked.

"Not so bad, Toby," he said. His big hat hid his face, but I could see his fingers working. When he blew the sawdust away, I saw the head of a horse carved into his stick.

"Wow!" I said.

"This is Paloma, the horse your grandmother and I had when we panned for gold."

"You really panned for gold?" I asked. Gramps was starting to look different to me. His hat didn't seem so big anymore. I sat down next to him as he worked.

"It was long before your time, Toby. Before your mother's, too," Gramps said. "Your Grandma Clara and I lived in an old canvas tent on the banks of a stream in the Sierra Nevada.* And no," he said, answering the unspoken question in my eyes, "we never did strike it rich. But Clara and I didn't mind. We made enough to get us to our next adventure."

"I suppose you went hunting for lost gold mines," I said jokingly.

"Now that's a whole other story," he said. ❖❖

---

* **Sierra Nevada:** a mountain range in eastern California

List the important parts of the passage.

If you can figure out what is important in the passage, you'll be able to state the main idea. On the lines below, write three important parts of the passage you just read.

3. _____

_____

4. _____

_____

5. _____

_____

Tip 4 **Look for a sentence that tells the main idea. If no main idea is stated, put it in your own words.**

Look back at the story. Is there a single sentence that tells the main idea?

6. Think about the important parts of the story you listed under Tip 3. Use them to write the main idea on the lines below.

_____

_____

_____

Look for the main idea in the answer choices.

You've written the main idea in your own words. Now see if you can find it in the answer choices.

7. What is the main idea of the story?
   Ⓐ Toby is learning how to whittle.
   Ⓑ Toby's grandfather once owned a horse.
   Ⓒ Toby is getting to know his grandfather.
   Ⓓ Toby's grandfather lived on a cattle ranch.

Look at choice A. Does the passage tell us that Toby is learning how to whittle? No. Choice A is not an idea in the passage.

Choice B tells us a little bit about Gramps, but it isn't the main idea.

Choice C states that Toby is getting to know his grandfather. This is the main idea of the story.

Choice D is a fact from the story. It helps us understand a little about Gramps, but it isn't the main idea.

Sample Main Idea Question

Directions: Answer the following question. Base your answer on the story "Getting to Know Gramps."

1. Which sentence BEST tells about this passage?
   Ⓐ Toby's grandfather tells him about a horse he owned long ago.
   Ⓑ Toby's grandfather whittles a horse's head on top of his walking stick.
   Ⓒ Toby's grandparents once lived in a tent next to a stream and panned for gold.
   Ⓓ Now that Gramps has come to live with him, Toby learns about his grandfather's life.

Additional Practice Questions

Directions: Now try answering some other types of questions about the story. You'll learn more about these question types in other lessons of this book.

2. Why does Gramps not seem to mind that he did not "strike it rich" as a gold miner?
   - Ⓐ He and Clara did not like panning for gold.
   - Ⓑ He earned enough money to do other things.
   - Ⓒ He bought a horse with the money he earned.
   - Ⓓ He had planned to go to work on a cattle ranch.

3. What does Gramps mean when he says, "Now that's a whole other story"?
   - Ⓐ He has another story to tell Toby.
   - Ⓑ The tales he's telling Toby are not true.
   - Ⓒ He wants Toby to write a story for him.
   - Ⓓ He doesn't know the answer to Toby's question.

4. Which of the following events happened FIRST?
   - Ⓐ Gramps came to live with Toby.
   - Ⓑ Gramps told Toby about his horse, Paloma.
   - Ⓒ Gramps worked as a foreman on a cattle ranch.
   - Ⓓ Gramps carved the head of a horse into his walking stick.

5. How does Toby get to know his grandfather? Use details and examples from the story to explain your answer.

   _____

   _____

   _____

   _____

   _____

   _____

Lesson 2

Details, Details, Details

Details are the facts and descriptions that add interest to a reading passage. Without them, reading would be terribly dull.

Practice Passage

Directions: Read the article "Bessie Smith: Empress of the Blues." It will help you understand the lesson.

Bessie Smith: Empress of the Blues

by Jules Highland

In 1894, Bessie Smith was born into a poor family in Chattanooga, Tennessee. As a little girl, she sang to the world while standing outside her family's run-down house. Her songs were simple, and her voice was strong and beautiful to hear.

Bessie performed in public for the first time when she was about eight years old. Her brother Andrew played his guitar while she danced and sang on a street corner in Chattanooga. People walking by tossed money to them.

When she was 18 years old, Bessie met a famous singer named Ma Rainey. "Let your soul do the singing," Ma told her. And Bessie did. Her sad songs told of the hard life she had lived and the troubles she had suffered.

Bessie sang a type of music called the *blues*. The blues grew out of the many different kinds of music sung and played by African Americans in the 1800s. Many blues songs are about loneliness and sorrow. Others are about people keeping their strength and sense of humor in times of trouble.

Bessie's music deeply touched the people who heard her sing. She was so popular in the 1920s that she became the highest paid African American entertainer in the country. From Detroit to New Orleans, traffic jams developed around theaters where she performed. Bessie's popularity helped bring the blues to a wider audience. The young singer soon became known as the "Empress of the Blues."

Bessie made more than 150 recordings during her lifetime. Her music <u>influenced</u> many other singers who came after her, and entertainers continue to learn from her recordings today. When Bessie died in 1937, a marker was placed on her grave. It reads, "The Greatest Blues Singer Will Never Stop Singing." ❖❖

Details Tips

Detail questions are usually the easiest types of questions to answer. Below are a few tips to help you answer detail questions about the passage you just read.

Tip 1   **Identify the main idea.**

The most important details are the ones that support the main idea. To understand which details are important, you first need to know the main idea of the passage.

1. What is the main idea of the article?

   _____

   _____

Tip 2   **Look for details that support the main idea.**

The main idea of a reading passage is like the roof of a house. A roof is supported by walls. The main idea of a passage is supported by details in the passage.

If a wall stands a few feet from the roof, it can't hold the roof up. In the same way, details that have nothing to do with the main idea can't support the main idea. If the details don't support the main idea, then those details aren't the most important ones.

2. In the graphic organizer below, write two more important details that support the main idea of the article.

Main Idea
Bessie Smith was a great blues singer.

Supporting Detail	Supporting Detail	Supporting Detail
Bessie's music deeply touched people.		

Identify key words in the question. Skim the passage to find the key words.

Look for the most important word or phrase (group of words) in the question. These words are usually easy to find when you skim the reading passage.

3. Read the question below. Circle key words or phrases that might help you find the answer in the article.

Where did Bessie FIRST earn money for performing?

Skimming means to run your eyes quickly over the reading material while looking for something. Skim the article "Bessie Smith" to find the key words you circled in the question above. Reread the sentences in the article containing those words.

Now read the question again. (It is reprinted below.) Then read the answer choices and choose the correct answer.

4. Where did Bessie FIRST earn money for performing?
   - Ⓐ at a theater in Detroit
   - Ⓑ outside her family's house
   - Ⓒ at a theater in Chattanooga
   - Ⓓ on a street corner in her hometown

To determine the order of events, identify key words in the answer choices.

Some detail questions may ask which event happened FIRST, NEXT, or LAST. To answer these questions, look for key words in the answer choices. Then skim the passage to find the key words.

Circle the key words in the following answer choices. Then go back to the article and reread the sentences containing those words.

5. Which of the following happened FIRST?
   - Ⓐ Bessie made more than 150 recordings.
   - Ⓑ Bessie met famous singer Ma Rainey.
   - Ⓒ Bessie became a highly-paid entertainer.
   - Ⓓ Bessie became known as "Empress of the Blues."

Now use the information you gathered to answer the question.

Sample Detail Questions

Directions: Answer the following questions. Base your answers on the article "Bessie Smith: Empress of the Blues."

1. How old was Bessie when she met Ma Rainey?
   - Ⓐ 8 years old
   - Ⓒ 20 years old
   - Ⓑ 18 years old
   - Ⓓ 37 years old

2. What happened to Bessie AFTER she met Ma Rainey?
   - Ⓐ She became even poorer.
   - Ⓑ She stopped singing sad songs.
   - Ⓒ She became a popular singer herself.
   - Ⓓ She never went back to Chattanooga.

3. Which of the following happened LAST?
   - Ⓐ Bessie met a famous female singer.
   - Ⓑ Bessie sang outside her family's house.
   - Ⓒ Bessie performed with her brother Andrew.
   - Ⓓ Bessie performed in theaters around the country.

Additional Practice Questions

Directions: Now try answering some other types of questions about the article. You'll learn more about these question types in other lessons of this book.

4. Which of the following statements is an OPINION?
   - Ⓐ "... her voice was strong and beautiful to hear."
   - Ⓑ "People walking by tossed money to them."
   - Ⓒ "Bessie sang a type of music called the *blues*."
   - Ⓓ "... she became the highest paid African American entertainer. ..."

5. What caused the traffic jams described in the article?
   - Ⓐ the people rushing to buy Bessie's records
   - Ⓑ the cars that brought Bessie's band to the theater
   - Ⓒ the people who tossed money to Bessie and Andrew
   - Ⓓ the crowds of people going to see Bessie's performances

6. What does the author mean by saying that Bessie *influenced* other singers?
   - Ⓐ Other singers refused to sing the blues.
   - Ⓑ Other singers placed a marker on her grave.
   - Ⓒ Other singers learned from the way Bessie sang.
   - Ⓓ Other singers tried to make as many recordings as Bessie.

Lesson 3

What's the Word?

Whether you're reading for school or for pleasure, you're bound (likely) to encounter (come across) an unfamiliar (strange) word or phrase once in a while. Don't get befuddled (confused). With a few simple strategies (plans of attack), you can decipher (figure out the meaning of) almost any word or phrase you're likely to meet.

Vocabulary Tips

Here are a few tips for figuring out the meanings of difficult words in a reading passage.

 Reread the sentence that contains the unknown word.

Some questions on the state test may ask about the meaning of a word in the passage. To answer these questions, go back to the passage and find the sentence in which the word appears.

Reread the sentence carefully. This will help you find the clues you need to figure out the meaning of the unfamiliar word.

You may also want to reread the paragraph surrounding the unknown word. Seeing the word in the context of the paragraph will give you even more clues to its meaning.

 Look for other words in the passage that have about the same meaning.

If you read carefully, you might find other words in the passage that have the same meaning as the unknown word or phrase.

Read the passage on the following page from *The Summer of the Swans* by Betsy Byars. It tells about a girl named Sara who enjoys watching movies on television.

She was good, too, at joining in the <u>dialogue</u> with the actors. When the cowboy would say something like, "Things are quiet around here tonight," she would join in with, "Yeah, *too* quiet," right on cue.

1. When a cowboy says something in a movie, what does Sara do?

_____

_____

_____

Think about what Sara does. Then answer the following question.

2. What does *dialogue* mean in this passage?
   Ⓐ fun
   Ⓑ talk
   Ⓒ action
   Ⓓ picture

The passage tells that a cowboy would "say something" and that Sara "would join in." To "say something" and to "join in" by speaking are both talking. You can probably guess that "dialogue" is a conversation—in other words, *talk*.

 Look for words in the passage that have the opposite meaning.

Sometimes the passage will give you clues to the opposite meaning of the unknown word. Read the following passage. Then answer numbers 3 and 4.

In the northeastern part of New Jersey, there are more people per square mile than in almost any other area of the United States. This heavily populated area is different from other parts of the state. The southeastern region, for example, is very <u>sparsely</u> populated.

3. Underline any words in the passage that mean the opposite of *sparsely*.

4. What does *sparsely* mean?
    Ⓐ lightly
    Ⓑ neatly
    Ⓒ busily
    Ⓓ strongly

 Look for less obvious clues to the meaning of the word.

Some vocabulary clues are more subtle (not immediately obvious). Read the passage below. Then answer numbers 5 and 6.

> Akira stood scratching his head; he was <u>perplexed</u>. He had left his social studies book on the kitchen table an hour ago. Now he couldn't find it anywhere. He looked under the table and in the pantry and even in the refrigerator. No book. His luck wasn't much better in the rest of the house, either. He retraced his steps, going over every inch of territory he had covered since he saw it last. *Now where is that thing?* he asked himself.

Think about how Akira feels about the missing book. Then answer the following questions.

5. What does *perplexed* mean in this passage?
    Ⓐ dirty
    Ⓑ lucky
    Ⓒ hungry
    Ⓓ puzzled

6. How do you know? Give clues from the passage to support your answer.

_____

_____

_____

Use "word parts" to figure out the meanings of words.

One way to figure out the meaning of an unknown word is to study the parts of the word. There are three kinds of "word parts" you should know about: prefixes, root words, and suffixes.

Prefixes are parts added onto the beginning of a **root word** (base word). A few common prefixes are shown below.

Prefix		Root Word		New Word
re- (again)	+	tell	=	**re**tell (tell again)
un- (not)	+	like	=	**un**like (not like)
mis- (wrong)	+	judge	=	**mis**judge (judge wrongly)

Suffixes are parts added onto the end of a root word. Here are a few suffixes you should know.

Root Word		Suffix		New Word
surf	+	**-er** (one who does)	=	surf**er** (one who surfs)
color	+	**-less** (without)	=	color**less** (without color)
hope	+	**-ful** (full of)	=	hope**ful** (full of hope)
happy	+	**-ness** (quality of)	=	happi**ness** (the quality of being happy)
enjoy	+	**-able** (able to)	=	enjoy**able** (able to be enjoyed)
careful	+	**-ly** (in a certain way or manner)	=	careful**ly** (in a careful manner)

Practice Activity

Directions: Answer numbers 7 through 12 by writing the meaning of each word on the lines provided. The first one has been done for you.

7. rewrite

   write again
   _____

8. careless

   _____

9. thoughtfulness

   _____

10. nervously

    _____

11. unbreakable

    _____

12. misunderstood

    _____

 Tip 6 **Look out for words with more than one meaning.**

Some words have more than one meaning. For example, you might eat *jam* on your toast for breakfast, *jam* your books into your backpack, and get into a traffic *jam*—all in the same morning.

To figure out the meanings of these types of words, you must pay close attention to the surrounding words and sentences. Try this tip on the following questions.

13. Read this sentence.

    Jonathan placed a pot of water on the <u>range</u>; soon he would have a half-dozen hard-boiled eggs.

    What does *range* mean in this sentence?
    - Ⓐ land for grazing
    - Ⓑ stove for cooking
    - Ⓒ a row or line of mountains
    - Ⓓ amounts between certain limits

    How do you know?

    _____

    _____

    _____

14. Read this sentence.

    The prices of computer games fall in a wide <u>range</u>, from $25 to $100.

    What does *range* mean in this sentence?
    - Ⓐ land for grazing
    - Ⓑ stove for cooking
    - Ⓒ a row or line of mountains
    - Ⓓ amounts between certain limits

    How do you know?

    _____

    _____

    _____

15. Read this sentence.

    Tobias's family raises cattle on a <u>range</u>.

    What does *range* mean in this sentence?
    - Ⓐ land for grazing
    - Ⓑ stove for cooking
    - Ⓒ a row or line of mountains
    - Ⓓ amounts between certain limits

    How do you know?

    _____

    _____

    _____

 Plug the answer choices into the sentence in place of the unknown word or phrase.

Try plugging the answer choices into the sentence in place of the unknown word or phrase. The one that makes the most sense in the passage should be the correct answer. (This is also a great way to check your work after choosing your answer using the other tips.)

Read the following passage.

    Gilly's heart <u>ached</u> with sorrow. Her best friend Monty was leaving Trenton to live on a ranch in Colorado. Would she ever get over the pain of his leaving?

16. What does *ached* mean in this passage?
    - Ⓐ hurt a lot
    - Ⓑ beat slowly
    - Ⓒ kept pounding
    - Ⓓ thumped loudly

Plug each answer choice into the passage in place of the word *ached*.

    Gilly's heart _____ with sorrow. Her best friend Monty was leaving Trenton to live on a ranch in Colorado. Would she ever get over the pain of his leaving?

Which choice makes the most sense in the passage? Why do you think so?

_____

_____

_____

_____

Practice Passage

Directions: Read the article "Little Brother of War." Then answer the questions that follow.

Little Brother of War

by Greta Anderson

1   Imagine an <u>ancient</u> sport something like modern soccer, played on a field with no boundaries and no time limits. The teams sometimes had as many as a thousand players on each side, and the goals were miles apart. It was a rough game that often lasted for two or three days, and it involved whole towns rushing at each other for a ball smaller than a baseball.

2   We call the game *lacrosse*, although the original players, North American Indians, called it "baggataway" or "tewaraathon." Men used the game to <u>condition</u> their bodies for war. When European settlers first saw lacrosse played in the 1800s, the Indians had already been playing it for almost a thousand years.

3   Lacrosse players try to move the ball by scooping it up, carrying it, and throwing it with a special playing stick. The object is to get the ball into a goal similar to a soccer goal.

4   Lacrosse got its name from early French Canadians. They thought the playing stick looked like a bishop's crosier[1]. The French words for "the crosier"—*la crosse*—eventually became the name of the sport.

---

[1]**crosier:** a curved pole that looks something like a shepherd's crook, carried by bishops as a symbol of responsibility toward their "flock" (or congregations).

5   The stick each player uses to catch, carry, and throw the ball is still called a "crosse." It consists of a shallow leather pocket at the end of a three- or four-foot staff. This pocket works something like a baseball glove. Players use it to catch balls coming toward them at high speeds. The long stick, or crosse, is the reason the ball travels so fast. It works as an extension of the player's throwing arm, similar to the way a baseball bat makes a batter's swinging arm longer.

6   The game, as the Indians played it, varied from tribe to tribe. The Seminoles had a version that used short sticks and a ball sewn together out of snapping turtle's skin. They had special matches of "stickball" during their green corn festival in early summer. The men <u>faced off</u> against the women. The women were allowed to catch, carry, and throw the ball with their hands if they didn't want to use a crosse. You can be sure there was a lot of teasing and good-natured arguing about the rules.

7   When the men played against the men, however, it was all-out war. Each player tried to physically injure as many opponents as possible before making a goal! In fact, the Cherokee called their version of the game "little brother of war."

8   As Europeans learned to play, the game became more and more like soccer. It was given set time periods and regulation-sized fields. Today's lacrosse uses <u>approximately</u> the same number of players as football and soccer: 10 players on men's teams and 12 players on women's. (Soccer and football each have 11 players on a team.) Lacrosse is played on a field about the same size and shape as a soccer field. The goal, however, is much smaller than a soccer goal.

9   As in soccer and football, the ball is moved down the field by passing and running. If someone "fumbles," anyone can scoop up the ball by using the sack end of the crosse. The tricky part is running down the field with the ball tucked inside the pocket. Players use a certain back-and-forth motion with the ball, called "cradling," as they run. If they didn't, the ball might fall out or be knocked out by an opponent.

10   Lacrosse is a game that requires endurance, speed, coordination, and guts. Although it's a lot of fun to play, lacrosse hasn't "taken off" like soccer, the world's most popular sport. Lacrosse is, however, one of Canada's favorite pastimes, second only to ice hockey. ❖❖

Sample Vocabulary Questions

Directions: Answer the following questions. Base your answers on the article "Little Brother of War."

1. What does *ancient* mean in paragraph 1?
   - Ⓐ very old
   - Ⓑ very fast
   - Ⓒ very difficult
   - Ⓓ very dangerous

2. What does *condition* mean in paragraph 2?
   - Ⓐ wash
   - Ⓑ paint
   - Ⓒ repair
   - Ⓓ train

3. What does *faced off* mean in paragraph 6?
   - Ⓐ teased
   - Ⓑ played
   - Ⓒ argued
   - Ⓓ coached

4. What does *approximately* mean in paragraph 8?
   - Ⓐ exactly
   - Ⓑ usually
   - Ⓒ about
   - Ⓓ sometimes

Additional Practice Questions

Directions: Now try answering some other types of questions about the article. You'll learn more about these question types in other lessons of this book.

5. Why did the author write the article "Little Brother of War"?
   - Ⓐ to tell about a game invented by American Indians
   - Ⓑ to tell about the lives of Seminole and Cherokee Indians
   - Ⓒ to persuade people to support a Canadian lacrosse team
   - Ⓓ to show readers the best way for soldiers to prepare for war

6. How is the shallow pocket of a crosse like a baseball glove?
   Ⓐ The player's hand is placed inside it.
   Ⓑ It extends the player's swinging arm.
   Ⓒ It is used to catch balls traveling very fast.
   Ⓓ It is used to cause another player to "fumble."

7. What are the MAIN differences between modern lacrosse and earlier American Indian versions of the game?

_____

_____

_____

_____

_____

_____

_____

_____

_____

Lesson 4

Be Your Own Reading Doctor

Good readers know how to make sure they understand what they're reading. As they read, they sometimes stop to give themselves a "reading checkup." If they find they don't understand, they have remedies to help cure their reading problem.

Reading Checkup Tips

The following tips will help you learn how to give yourself a "reading checkup."

 **Determine the main idea.**

First ask yourself, "What is this passage mainly about?" Getting the big picture is one of the most important parts of understanding what you read.

Practice Passage

Directions: Read the first paragraph of the story "Taking Aim," below. Then answer number 1.

TAKING AIM
BY LES FIRPO

   "This isn't Camp Good Hope, it's Camp No Hope," Narada wrote in a letter to his parents. "I just can't do anything right here. On our trail ride, my horse <u>bolted</u> away from the group and ran for the barn. Then when we played softball, I struck out three times in one game. And when we went canoeing on the lake, I fell overboard. Don't worry, I'm fine," he added, "but I sure was embarrassed when the counselors had to fish me out of the water. Nothing I do is any good. Are you sure I can't go home early?" He dropped the letter off at the camp mail box and trudged back to his cabin to wash up for lunch.

1. What do you think this story will be mainly about?

_____

_____

_____

Tip 2 **Ask questions as you read.**

As you read, stop regularly to ask yourself, "Do I understand what the author is saying? Does this make sense?" You may also want to ask yourself other questions about the passage.

Directions: Continue reading the story "Taking Aim." As you read, notice the questions shown to the right of the story. Write one or two questions of your own next to the story as you read.

Aaron, Narada's counselor, was in the cabin checking off the list of names as the boys got ready for lunch. Aaron said, "What's with the glum look, Narada?"

"I hate this place," Narada said. "I can't seem to do anything right. Everything I do goes wrong. Maybe I shouldn't have come here."

"Or maybe you just haven't tried the right things yet," Aaron said as they walked over to the mess hall together. Aaron was tall, strong, and well liked by the campers.

That's easy for him to say, Narada thought. *He does everything well. I wish I could be like him.*

Aaron continued, "Sure, there are some activities that you have trouble with. No one can be good at everything. Your job is to find out what you *are* good at. Everyone is good at something. You will be, too."

"I doubt it," Narada said. He bent over and picked up a rock from the path. He threw it at the flagpole across the courtyard. *Twang!* the flagpole sounded as the rock hit.

"Can you do that again?" Aaron asked.

"Sure," Narada said. "It's no big deal. Anybody can do it." He found another stone and threw it at the flagpole.

What does "glum" mean?

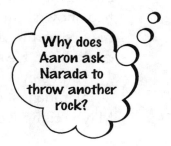

Why does Aaron ask Narada to throw another rock?

Twang! came the sound again.

Then Aaron picked up a stone and threw it toward the flagpole. It missed by several feet. "Well, I guess anybody can't do it," Aaron chuckled. "I certainly can't."

Narada laughed, too. He was starting to feel a little better.

"I want you to come with me after lunch," Aaron told Narada. "There's something I'd like you to try."

In the mess hall, Narada wolfed down his sausage pizza as fast as he could. Then he stuffed his chocolate cupcake into his mouth and quickly carried his tray to the cleanup window. He couldn't wait to find out what Aaron wanted him to try.

Aaron was talking to some other counselors near the exit. When he saw Narada, he waved and pointed to the doorway of the mess hall. Then he left his group of friends and took the young boy outside.

Will Aaron teach Narada something new?

Together they walked to a long field where big, round, paper targets were tacked to bales of straw. The counselor went into an old wooden shed and brought out a bow and six feathered arrows.

Aaron showed Narada how to hold the bow. He went through all the steps of shooting an arrow. He started by explaining how to set the arrow onto the bow's arrow rest, place the bowstring into the arrow notch, and pull the arrow and bowstring back together until the feathers touched the cheek.

Aaron took the bow into his powerful arms. He set an arrow on the string just as he had shown Narada. When he let go of the bowstring, the arrow shot into the air. It flew high and straight, and its tip struck the white edge of the paper, just outside the target's outer ring. It was a miss. No points for Aaron.

"Now you try, Narada," Aaron said.

The bow felt good in Narada's hands—comfortable, as if he'd always held one. Narada placed an arrow on the arrow rest, notched it into the bowstring, and pulled the string back just as Aaron had shown him. Suddenly he felt very excited. He aimed his first arrow at the center of the target. Narada knew he could hit it. He smiled, then shot the arrow.

"Bull's-eye!" Aaron shouted.

Narada just grinned and picked up another arrow. Maybe camp would be fun, after all. ❖❖

As you read, stop and retell or summarize.

When reading a fictional story, stop occasionally to **retell** the main events of the story to yourself. Retelling will help you make sure you are understanding what is happening in the story.

When reading a nonfiction article, stop and **summarize** it by listing the most important points in your mind. These are the points the author uses to support the main idea. Summarizing will help make the meaning of the article clear.

 After you read, go back and skim.

After you finish reading, go back to the passage and skim for the main events or the main points. Retell the main events or summarize the main points to make sure you understand the passage.

2.   Retell the important events of the story "Taking Aim" on the lines below.

_____

_____

_____

_____

_____

_____

_____

_____

Reread the difficult parts.

If you have difficulty retelling or summarizing, you might be having trouble understanding some part of the passage. Go back and reread any part of the passage that seems difficult. Then try summarizing the main points or retelling the main events again.

3. Did you find some parts of the story difficult to understand? If so, go back and mark those parts with your pencil. Then read those parts of the story again.

Tip 6 **Figure out the meanings of difficult words.**

If you don't understand some of the words, first try using clues from the passage to figure out their meanings. If that doesn't work, look up the definitions to unfamiliar words in a dictionary. (You will not be allowed to use a dictionary on the state test. But you can use the tips you learned in Lesson 3 to help you figure out the meanings of unfamiliar words.)

Tip 7 **Keep reading.**

If part of the passage still seems confusing, don't be discouraged. Just keep reading. Something farther on in the passage might make the meaning clear.

Tip 8 **Link your reading to your own experiences.**

Reading is more fun when we relate it to our lives. For example, Narada's story may remind you of when *you* went to camp. Or it may remind you of a time you felt you could do nothing well. The story may even remind you of a time you learned something new.

Use what you know.

You have been busy learning your whole life. You can bring what you've learned to your reading.

For example, imagine you did not understand what was happening in the story when Narada was learning to use the bow. If you have ever tried archery (the sport of shooting at a target with a bow and arrow), you can use your knowledge to help you understand that part of the story.

 ## Check other sources.

Learning more about the topic of the passage will help you to better understand the passage. For example, to help you understand the story "Taking Aim," you might read an encyclopedia article on archery. (You can learn more about using resources in Lesson 13.)

 ## Listen to the passage read aloud.

Sometimes it helps to hear a passage read aloud. If you don't understand a passage, try reading it aloud to yourself. Or ask someone to read it aloud to you. You will be surprised how much *hearing* helps with *understanding*.

 ## Talk with others about what you are reading.

Another way to better understand a passage is to talk with someone else who has read it. Ask the person any questions you have about the passage. Also ask that person what they liked, what they disliked, and why.

Practice Activity

Directions: Discuss the story "Taking Aim" with one of your classmates. Record their answers to numbers 4 through 8 on the lines provided.

4. Did Narada's story remind you of any experiences you have had? If so, explain.

_____

_____

_____

5. What did you like about the story? Why?

_____

_____

_____

6. What did you dislike about the story? Why?

_____

_____

_____

7. Did you learn anything new from the story?

_____

_____

_____

8. Make up a question of your own to ask your classmate.

   Your question:

   _____

   _____

   Your classmate's answer:

   _____

   _____

You may wish to write questions and answers such as these in your training log. To learn more about using a training log, see page 3.

Additional Practice Questions

Directions: Now try answering some other types of questions about the story. You'll learn more about these question types in other lessons of this book.

1. What is the main reason Narada dislikes Camp Good Hope at the beginning of the story?
   - Ⓐ He does not like his camp cabin.
   - Ⓑ He misses his parents back home.
   - Ⓒ He thinks he can't do anything well.
   - Ⓓ He gets hurt when he falls out of a canoe.

2. What does *bolted* mean?
   - Ⓐ closed tightly
   - Ⓑ sat up straight
   - Ⓒ attacked wildly
   - Ⓓ moved suddenly

3. Why does Aaron show Narada how to use a bow and arrow?
   - Ⓐ He wants to show Narada how to hit a flagpole.
   - Ⓑ He wants to help Narada find something he is good at.
   - Ⓒ He wants to introduce Narada to the other counselors.
   - Ⓓ He wants Narada to help him set up the targets on the hay bales.

4. How are Narada's feelings about himself DIFFERENT at the end of the story?
   - Ⓐ He feels worse because he has made another mistake.
   - Ⓑ He feels no different because nothing has changed for him.
   - Ⓒ He feels better because he has found something that he does well.
   - Ⓓ He feels better because his parents are allowing him to come home early.

5. What lesson does Narada learn in the story? Use details from the story to explain your answer.

_____

_____

_____

_____

_____

_____

_____

_____

_____

_____

_____

_____

Reading Between the Lines

Lesson 5

People and Places

The people in a made-up story are called **characters**. Sometimes the characters are animals that act like people. Characters can even be imaginary things like talking shoes or a friendly monster. Stories usually have one or two really important characters and several less important ones.

Where and when the story takes place is called the **setting**. Sometimes a story may happen in more than one place or time. Each time the location of the story changes or the time switches, we say there has been a change of setting.

Character and Setting Tips

The following tips will help you think about the characters and settings in a story.

 Tip 1   **Look for details about the characters.**

Finding out about characters is mostly a matter of paying attention to details. Read the passage on the following page. Then answer numbers 1 through 8.

Kelly marched across the playground toward Junior Becker. She was the smallest student in her class, but she seemed about as small as a thunderstorm at that moment. Just the look in her dark brown eyes would've been enough to knock most kids over. She'd rolled up the sleeves of her baggy black sweatshirt and was pulling her little brother Ben behind her. Ben was still wiping the mashed peanut butter and jelly sandwich from his blond hair. Kelly's friends—Mara, Shelley, and Alisha—were there, too, running behind her, telling her to forget about it.

"Not until Junior apologizes," Kelly said.

Just ahead, by the dumpster, stood Junior—thick as a tree trunk and surrounded by his goofy friends.

1. How many friends are with Kelly? _____

2. What does Kelly look like?

   _____

   _____

3. Tell one detail about Ben.

   _____

   _____

4. Tell one detail about Junior.

   _____

   _____

5. Which character is angry?
   Ⓐ Mara
   Ⓑ Kelly
   Ⓒ Alisha
   Ⓓ Junior Becker

6. Who is pulling Ben by the hand?
   - Ⓐ Kelly
   - Ⓑ Alisha
   - Ⓒ Shelley
   - Ⓓ Junior Becker

7. How old is Ben?
   - Ⓐ older than Kelly
   - Ⓑ older than Junior
   - Ⓒ younger than Kelly
   - Ⓓ the same age as Kelly

8. What are Kelly's friends doing?
   - Ⓐ teasing Kelly and Ben
   - Ⓑ telling Junior he should apologize
   - Ⓒ telling Junior to leave Kelly and Ben alone
   - Ⓓ telling Kelly to forget something that has happened

 Tip 2   **"Listen" as the author introduces you to the characters.**

In real life, you might learn about someone by listening to other people talk. When you read, you can get to know the characters by "listening" to what the author has to say about them.

Read the passage below from *Encyclopedia Brown and the Case of the Mysterious Handprints* by Donald J. Sobol. Then answer numbers 9 and 10.

Only his parents and teachers called him by his real name, Leroy. Everyone else called him Encyclopedia.

An encyclopedia is a book or set of books filled with facts from A to Z. So was Encyclopedia's head. He had read more books than anyone in Idaville, and he never forgot what he read. His pals insisted that he was better than a library.

9. Which word BEST describes Leroy?
   - Ⓐ rude
   - Ⓑ smart
   - Ⓒ carefree
   - Ⓓ friendly

10. According to the passage, which sentence tells how Leroy's friends MOST LIKELY feel about him?

   Ⓐ They are proud to be his friends.

   Ⓑ They are jealous of his good memory.

   Ⓒ They don't believe he can remember things.

   Ⓓ They want to prove that he can forget things.

 Pay attention to how the characters act.

You can learn a lot about characters by how they act in different situations. Read the following passage from *The Beast in Ms. Rooney's Room* by Patricia Reilly Giff. It tells about a boy named Richard Best on the first day of school. The girl who sits across from him has just smiled at Richard.

> He frowned at her. Then he pulled in his breath. Sniffing loudly, he stuck the eraser end of his new pencil up his nose.
> He shook his head. The pencil swung back and forth gently.
> The girl looked as if she were going to throw up.
> Good.

Now answer numbers 11 and 12.

11. What did Richard do AFTER the girl smiled at him?

   Ⓐ He threw up.

   Ⓑ He gave her his eraser.

   Ⓒ He stuck a pencil in his nose.

   Ⓓ He asked to borrow her pencil.

12. What do Richard's actions MOST LIKELY say about him?

   Ⓐ He has a cold.

   Ⓑ He is a friendly boy.

   Ⓒ He likes to upset people.

   Ⓓ He likes the smell of pencils.

Tip 4 **Notice how the characters are alike or different from each other.**

Sometimes an author will compare characters in the story. This can help the reader understand how the characters are alike or different from each other.

Read the following passage from *How Juan Got Home* by Peggy Mann.

> Juan kept talking almost nonstop all the way. He had so much talk inside him it seemed he just couldn't get it all said.
>
> Carlos spoke very little. When they had finished piling the boxes in a corner of the basement, Carlos explained why he always answered Juan in such short sentences. He knew very little Spanish.

13. Fill in the diagram to show one way in which Juan and Carlos are different from each other.

Juan	Carlos

Tip 5 **Notice how characters change during the story.**

In some stories, characters stay pretty much the same from beginning to end. In other stories, you will see a big change in some of the characters.

Read the passage below. Then answer numbers 14 and 15.

> Andrew wasn't embarrassed anymore. He began to enjoy his morning walks to school with Susan. She didn't seem half as giggly and scatter-brained as she used to before she pitched the Red Dogs to a 7-1 win. He noticed, too, that her red hair didn't seem quite as wild and fiery as it had last week. Even her freckles seemed to have disappeared. Maybe he'd invite her to stop at The Hut and have a soda with him on the way home. He didn't care what the rest of the guys said. Susan was turning out to be a pretty neat neighbor—and the best ball player on the team!

14. Which character or set of characters makes the BIGGEST change in the passage?

   Ⓐ Susan

   Ⓑ Andrew

   Ⓒ the Red Dogs

   Ⓓ the "rest of the guys"

15. In what way does this character change? Use details from the passage in your answer.

_____

_____

_____

_____

_____

Tip 6 **Look for details that tell you where and when the story takes place.**

Read the paragraph below from *Tornado!* by Walter R. Brown and Norman D. Anderson. Then answer the questions that follow.

   The trim fifteen-year-old girl glanced over her shoulder at the tumbling, swirling mass of black clouds that nearly covered the Michigan sky. It was the third week in March, 1976.

16. Where does the story take place?

_____

17. When does the story take place?

_____

18. What event is taking place at the time of the story?

_____

Tip 7 **If the story has more than one setting, notice how the settings are alike or different.**

Authors often set a story in more than one place. They may finish writing about one place completely and move on to another, or they may switch back and forth between places throughout the story.

Many times authors will develop a story by moving the settings forward and backward in time. For example, a story may start out by describing an adult character, and then flash back to when that person was a child.

Practice Passage

Directions: Read the story "The Wall." Then answer the questions that follow.

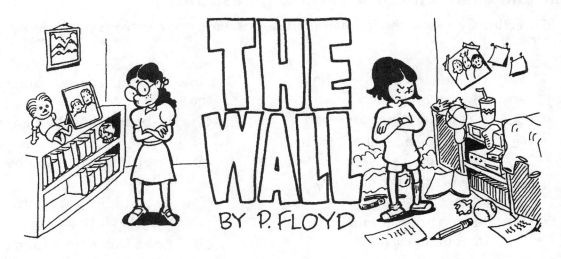

THE WALL BY P. FLOYD

    Shawna and Diana shared a bedroom. They were sisters, but they were as different as two sisters could be.

    Shawna always put her things away. She liked to clean her room, then lie on her bed and read. But Diana always made a mess of everything. She left books, shoes, and games all over the place. She liked to listen to very loud music.

    The two girls were always fighting.

    "I'm tired of having your things all over the room!" Shawna would say. "And turn down that music!"

    "I'm tired of you picking up my things!" Diana would say. "I don't touch your things."

    Then one day Shawna had an idea. "Why don't we put a line across the floor?" she said. "We'll pretend it's a wall. You can stay on your side of the room. I'll stay on my side."

They found a big roll of tape. Then they put a line across the middle of the room.

It didn't work. Diana still left her things on Shawna's side of the room. Shawna still picked up Diana's things. The tape just wasn't enough, so they put up a row of chairs. Next, they pulled their big bookcases into the middle of the room. At last, they could both do what they wanted.

The first night, Shawna said, "Hey, are you still there?"

The next night, Diana said, "Can I come see you? I miss you."

The third night, Shawna said, "This is a dumb idea. I don't like it."

"I hate it too," Diana said. "Maybe we could just try to get along."

"That sounds good to me," Shawna said. ❖❖

Sample Character and Setting Questions

Directions: Answer the following questions. Base your answers on the story "The Wall."

1. How do the girls usually behave when they are together?
   - Ⓐ They build things together.
   - Ⓑ They argue a lot about their differences.
   - Ⓒ They play music and have fun together.
   - Ⓓ They do not pay much attention to each other.

2. How does Shawna feel about Diana leaving her things lying around?
   - Ⓐ sad
   - Ⓑ glad
   - Ⓒ angry
   - Ⓓ jealous

3. How does the setting change in the story?
   - Ⓐ The bedroom is divided in half.
   - Ⓑ The girls move to another bedroom.
   - Ⓒ The bedroom goes from messy to clean.
   - Ⓓ The bedroom goes from clean to messy.

4. How do the girls' feelings toward each other change during the story?
   - Ⓐ from happy to sad
   - Ⓑ from mad to bored
   - Ⓒ from sad to puzzled
   - Ⓓ from angry to friendly

5. How are Shawna and Diana DIFFERENT? Use details and examples from the story to explain your answer.

_____

_____

_____

_____

Additional Practice Questions

Directions: Now try answering some other types of questions about the story. You'll learn more about these question types in other lessons of this book.

6. What is MOST LIKELY to happen next in the story?
   - Ⓐ The girls will start to fight.
   - Ⓑ The girls will take down the wall.
   - Ⓒ The girls will get separate bedrooms.
   - Ⓓ The girls will start to like the same things.

7. Why did the author write the story "The Wall"?
   - Ⓐ to teach people how to arrange a bedroom
   - Ⓑ to persuade people to clean their bedrooms
   - Ⓒ to entertain people with a story about sisters
   - Ⓓ to teach people to talk to their parents about problems

8. Why doesn't the wall work for Diana and Shawna? Use details from the story in your answer.

_____

_____

_____

_____

Lesson 6

The Plot Is Where the Action Is

A story doesn't really get going until something happens. These happenings are called the story's **plot**.

Plot Tips

In this lesson you will learn how to find the main problems in the story. You will also learn how to follow the important events, make predictions about what will happen next, and understand how the main problems are solved.

Tip 1 ***Look for the story's main idea.***

When a writer comes up with a plot, he or she has a plan in mind. This plan can be stated as a main idea. For example, the sentence below could have been the plan for the story about a certain famous superhero.

> A baby from a doomed planet grows up on Earth, finds out that he has superpowers, and uses them to help people.

Do you recognize this as the plan for the story of Superman?

Tip 2 ***Find the problems in the story.***

Good stories don't have to be about superheroes. And the action in them doesn't have to involve saving the earth to be interesting. Even the lives of ordinary people can be the subject of exciting stories, *if* they're well told. The plot makes all the difference.

In most stories, the characters have some sort of problem (sometimes called the **conflict**) that needs to be solved. Problems are an important part of a plot—they get the story going. There may be one or two big problems in the beginning and several smaller problems along the way.

Read the following passage from *Ramona and Her Father* by Beverly Cleary. Then answer number 1.

Mrs. Quimby looked at the cold creamed cauliflower with distaste, returned it to the refrigerator, and reached for a can of green beans before she noticed her silent and worried daughters watching her for clues as to what might be wrong.

Mrs. Quimby turned and faced Beezus and Ramona. "Girls, you might as well know. Your father has lost his job."

1. What is the MAIN problem in the passage?
    - Ⓐ The girls' father has lost his job.
    - Ⓑ The refrigerator needs cleaning.
    - Ⓒ The girls are watching for clues.
    - Ⓓ The creamed cauliflower is cold.

 Tip 3 **Decide who is involved in the problem.**

The main character will always face problems. That's just the way it goes. Sometimes the problem will be with another character, like a pesky elf, a stern teacher, or the neighborhood bully. Sometimes the problem will be with a thing, like a broken invention or a difficult test. And sometimes the problem will be within the character: *Should she tell her parents that she scraped their car with her bike? Or should she be quiet and hope they don't find out?*

Read the following sentences from *The One in the Middle is the Green Kangaroo* by Judy Blume. The story tells about a boy who has an older brother and a younger sister.

Freddy thought a lot about being the one in the middle. But there was nothing he could do about it. He felt like the peanut butter part of a sandwich, squeezed between Mike and Ellen.

2. What is Freddy's problem?
    - Ⓐ He does not like his brother and sister.
    - Ⓑ His brother and sister are squeezing him too hard.
    - Ⓒ He does not want to eat his peanut butter sandwich.
    - Ⓓ He does not like being the middle child in his family.

3. Freddy's problem is with which of the following?
    - Ⓐ his parents
    - Ⓑ his own feelings
    - Ⓒ his sister Ellen
    - Ⓓ his brother Mike

Tip 4 **Look for the main events.**

As you read a story, look for the main events. These are the most important events in the story, the ones that keep the plot moving.

Practice Passage

Directions: Read the following passage. As you read, ask yourself, "What problems do the characters face?" and "What are the most important events in this story?"

Terror in Touchstone House
by Nick Liakouras

Nancy held the flashlight while the twins, Tony and Noreen, crawled along the edge of the dark, spooky room. They moved slowly, feeling among the scattered books that lay about on the dusty floorboards.

"It has to be here—in this old library room," Nancy said, shivering. "Martin heard the man on the bus say that it would be hidden in Touchstone House until tomorrow morning. We have to find it *tonight!* Someone's bound to come back for it as soon as the sun comes up."

Dry boards squeaked as the children moved slowly across the old, wobbly floor.

"Over here, Nancy," Tony whispered. "Shine the flashlight down here. I think I've found something."

Nancy slid the pool of light to a spot just in front of Tony and Noreen. She gasped as the twins jumped to their feet with a strange scream, a scream that sounded more like a grunt.

"What is it?" Nancy asked.

"I don't know," Noreen said in a shaky voice. "I don't know. But it has yellow eyes, and it crawled into that hole in the floor."

"Let's get out of here," Tony whispered, running his hands along the dark wall, trying to find the door.

They stumbled across the empty library room, then ran along the dark hallway, down the crumbling front steps, and out into the moonlight.

Stopping in the shadows outside the iron entrance gate, the three detectives were quiet—except for the wild thumping of their hearts. ❖❖

4. What is the MAIN problem in the passage?
    Ⓐ The library room is dusty and empty.
    Ⓑ The floor of Touchstone House is old and wobbly.
    Ⓒ The children must find something before morning.
    Ⓓ An animal is crawling into a hole in the floorboards.

Use what you know about the characters to predict what will happen next.

The problems in a story create excitement as you anxiously turn the pages to see how the characters will solve them. If you know the characters well, you may be able to predict what will happen next. If the main character is a smart detective caught in a dangerous situation, chances are he or she will find a way out.

When making a prediction, don't make wild guesses. Base your answer on what you already know from the passage. A character's personality will affect the kinds of actions he or she takes. For example, if a character regularly does nice things for people, don't expect him or her to suddenly do something mean in the end.

5. What will the children PROBABLY do next in the story "Terror in Touchstone House"?
   Ⓐ They will hide inside the house until morning.
   Ⓑ They will ask to have the old house torn down.
   Ⓒ They will overcome their fear and continue their search.
   Ⓓ They will ask the person arriving the next morning to help them.

 Notice how the problem is solved.

In many stories, the problem is solved by the time you reach the end.

Directions: Continue reading the story "Terror in Touchstone House." Notice how the children solve their problem in this scene.

> "Now what?" Nancy asked in a hoarse whisper.
> "I have to think," Tony said, lowering himself to both knees just as the moon dipped behind a large, gray cloud. "Why should we run from a little thing with yellow eyes? We'll have to go back. If we don't get the map first, there's gonna be real trouble."
> "Can't we wait until morning?" Noreen wanted to know.
> "Get real, Noreen!" Tony snapped. "Do you want somebody to find it before we do?"
> "Not really, but that place gives me the creeps," Noreen whispered.
> "All right," Nancy said. "Both of you, be calm. We have to try it one more time. Come on. The moon's out again. Quick! Let's run for the door."
> They paused momentarily, then shot for the entrance steps and the great oaken door that led to the crumbling interior of Touchstone House. They stopped just inside the foyer, and Tony checked quickly up and down Brookwood Avenue before closing the door.

"Give me the flashlight, Nancy, and you and Noreen stay right behind me," Tony said, with much greater authority than he really felt.

The nervous group climbed the noisy stairs to the second floor library. Pausing at the half-open door, they waited while Tony scanned the empty room with the flashlight. He tensed momentarily, then relaxed, laughing softly.

"There's our friend, Mr. Yellow Eyes," he said, centering the light on a young, gray squirrel and watching the yellow beam reflect in its tiny eyes. The startled animal, frozen with fear, sat up, stared at the intruders momentarily, then scurried toward the hole in the library floor.

"It must have a nest under the floorboards," Nancy said. She bent down and peeked into the hole. Inside lay tiny shreds of torn paper and the tattered remains of an aging document. "It looks like Mr. Yellow Eyes has found the perfect material to line his nest," she said.

Tony shined the light onto the worn paper. "It's the map," he said, snatching it breathlessly and observing the places where whole chunks had been eaten away.

As they huddled to study their discovery, the great entrance door to Touchstone House squeaked open far below them and then closed with a thunderous boom. ❖❖

6. How do the detectives solve the problem of the missing map?

_____

_____

_____

_____

_____

_____

Not all stories have tidy endings. In some stories, the main problem isn't solved. Instead, the main character learns something new about herself or about the world that helps her understand her problem.

Sample Plot Questions

Directions: Answer the following questions. Base your answers on the story "Terror in Touchstone House."

1. Why do the children run from the house in the beginning of the story?
   - Ⓐ Their flashlight does not work.
   - Ⓑ They see something with yellow eyes.
   - Ⓒ The floorboards make squeaky noises.
   - Ⓓ They hear someone coming into the house.

2. What are the main events in the story?

   _____

   _____

   _____

   _____

   _____

   _____

   _____

   _____

   _____

Additional Practice Questions

Directions: Now try answering some other types of questions about the story. You'll learn more about these question types in other lessons in this book.

3. According to Nancy, where does Martin get his information about the location of the map?
   Ⓐ from Tony
   Ⓑ from Mr. Yellow Eyes
   Ⓒ from the man on the bus
   Ⓓ from the owner of Touchstone House

4. Why does Tony laugh after he scans the library with the flashlight?
   Ⓐ The map they are searching for is being used as a nest.
   Ⓑ Someone has already taken the map out of the library.
   Ⓒ What had scared them before turns out to be a squirrel.
   Ⓓ Someone comes in through the front door of Touchstone House.

5. This story might be found in which type of book?
   Ⓐ mystery
   Ⓑ nonfiction
   Ⓒ biography
   Ⓓ science fiction

Lesson 7

Alike and Different

To **compare** two things is to show how they are alike and different. In this lesson, you will learn to compare things such as characters, settings, events, and ideas. You also will learn to notice when an author compares things in a story or article.

The following passage shows similarities and differences in the way a boy named Henry and his dog Ribsy walk home after school during the week. It is from *Henry Huggins* by Beverly Cleary.

> Every afternoon after school Ribsy waited for Henry under a fir tree in the corner of the school yard. Four days a week they ran home the shortest way, past the park, up the hill, and through the vacant lot.
>
> On Fridays, however, they walked home the long way round past the Rose City Drugstore, the Supermarket, the Ideal Barber Shop, and the Lucky Dog Pet Shop.

1. What is DIFFERENT about the way Henry and Ribsy go home on Fridays?
   - Ⓐ They go past the park.
   - Ⓑ They take a longer path.
   - Ⓒ They meet under a fir tree.
   - Ⓓ They go through a vacant lot.

2. How is the walk home on Fridays the SAME as the walk home on the other days of the week?
   - Ⓐ They go home together.
   - Ⓑ They always stop at the pet shop.
   - Ⓒ They go home as fast as they can.
   - Ⓓ They walk past the Supermarket.

Comparison Tips

Following are tips to help you make comparisons.

 Look for clue words that tell when things are being compared.

The table below contains some words and phrases (groups of words). These are clues that tell you the writer is making a comparison.

Similarities	Differences
alike	but
both	however
just as	instead of
similar	not the same as
the same as	on the other hand

3. Read the following passage from *The Amazing Bo Jackson* by Randi Hacker. It tells about professional athlete Bo Jackson's early baseball career. As you read, underline the clue words that show a comparison.

   Bo's life in the minor leagues wasn't as glamorous as it might have been if he had decided to play pro football. Instead of riding in limousines and eating expensive food, he found himself riding for 15 hours in a bus and eating greasy hamburgers.

4. How did Bo's life as a minor league baseball player compare to what it would have been like as a professional football player?
   - Ⓐ He had to travel farther.
   - Ⓑ His life wasn't as comfortable.
   - Ⓒ He didn't get to eat as much food.
   - Ⓓ He was able to purchase his own bus.

> **Tip 2** **Look for other words that show direct comparisons, such as "bigger," "smallest," "more," and "less."**

Words that show a direct comparison are often the easiest to recognize. They also help you know how many things are being compared. Comparison words ending in *-er* compare only two things. Comparison words ending in *-est* compare three or more things.

The passage below is from *Dogsong* by Gary Paulsen. It describes two kinds of ice found in Alaska.

5. Circle the comparison words in the passage. Then underline any other clue words that tell you a comparison is being made.

> Sea ice is not the same as fresh-water ice. The salt-water ice is stronger, more elastic, isn't as slippery. Also the sea ice moves all the time, even when it is thick.

6. What two things are being compared in the passage?

    _____

    _____

Notice that sea ice is also called "salt-water ice" in the passage. The author tells four ways that sea ice (salt-water ice) is different from fresh-water ice. Fill in the blanks to finish the comparisons below.

7. Sea ice is _____ than fresh-water ice.

8. Sea ice is _____ than fresh-water ice.

9. Sea ice is not as _____ as fresh-water ice.

10. Fresh-water ice doesn't _____ all the time like sea ice does.

Tip 3 **If there are no clue words, look for details that show comparisons.**

Some comparisons are made just by giving detailed descriptions. The following passage from *Kevin's Grandma* by Barbara Williams does this. In the story, Kevin is the narrator's friend.

> On my birthday my grandma takes me out to lunch. Then we go shopping. She buys me any toy I want.
>
> On Kevin's birthday his grandma takes him in an airplane. He watches from the window while she goes skydiving.

11. Who is being compared in this story?
    Ⓐ Kevin and his grandma
    Ⓑ the narrator and his grandma
    Ⓒ the narrator and Kevin's grandma
    Ⓓ Kevin's grandma and the narrator's grandma

12. On their birthdays, what do Kevin and the narrator do ALIKE?
    Ⓐ go out to lunch
    Ⓑ fly in an airplane
    Ⓒ go shopping for a new toy
    Ⓓ spend time with their grandmothers

Tip 4 **Draw a chart to show similarities and differences.**

A chart can help you organize information so that comparisons are easier to make. Read the following information about professional wrestler Andre the Giant. It is from *Kings of the Ring: An Inside Guide to Pro Wrestling* by Joe Bosko.

> *Everything* about Andre is BIG. His fingers are so large that you could slip a silver dollar through one of his rings. By comparison, William "The Refrigerator" Perry's* fingers are tiny—you can only fit a half dollar through one of his rings. Andre's wrist is almost twelve inches around. That's an average-size wrist—for a gorilla. Most human wrists are about seven inches around.

* William Perry, a retired professional football player, was known as "The Refrigerator" because of his very large size.

13. Finish filling in the unshaded parts of the chart with information from the passage.

How Andre the Giant Compares to Others

Name	Finger Size	Wrist Size
Andre the Giant	Wears a ring large enough to fit a silver dollar through	12 inches around
William "The Refrigerator" Perry		
Gorilla		
Average Human		

14. Whose finger size would MOST LIKELY be the SMALLEST?
   - Ⓐ a gorilla
   - Ⓑ an average human
   - Ⓒ Andre the Giant
   - Ⓓ William Perry

15. How does Andre's wrist compare to that of an average gorilla?
   - Ⓐ It is slightly larger.
   - Ⓑ It is slightly smaller.
   - Ⓒ It is about the same size.
   - Ⓓ It is about half the size.

Practice Passage

Directions: Read the article "Don't Smile at a Crocodile." Then answer the questions that follow.

Don't Smile at a Crocodile

by Yolanda Plummer

"See you later, alligator," your cousin says.

"After a while, crocodile," you reply.

You and your cousin aren't all that different. Sure, she's three inches taller than you, and judging by your parents' heights, you're never going to catch up to her. Her hair is brown; yours is blonde. Her nose is long and narrow; yours is short with freckles. When you go to the pool, she likes to swim, and you like to float on your back or play "dead man." But when it comes down to it, you've got a lot in common. After all, you're part of the same family.

American crocodiles and American alligators have a lot in common, too. For starters, they're part of the same *Crocodylia* (KROCK-uh-DIL-ee-uh) family. They are the only two members of that family in the United States. They are similar in many ways. Both have long, low, cigar-shaped bodies, short, stubby legs, and powerful tails that they use for swimming. Also, they both have tough hides, sharp teeth, and long snouts.

But there are some basic, easy-to-remember differences between the alligator and the crocodile. The crocodile's snout is narrow and comes to a point. The alligator's snout is broader and rounded on the end. The alligator is smaller, eight to ten feet compared to the crocodile's twelve. The alligator is also more friendly—or at least it puts up with humans better. Crocodiles will attack without being disturbed, unlike alligators, which are usually more peaceful. Also, crocodiles are faster and more active.

The prehistoric granddaddies of today's *crocodilians* were alive during the age of the dinosaurs. They haven't changed much since then, although there used to be many more kinds, including a 50-foot model that may have helped put the dinos out of business!

Crocodiles and alligators have always lived in fresh water—rivers, lakes, and marshes—not in the salty water of the sea or ocean. Their water can be muddy, but it has to be warm. The American crocodile is found in the West Indies,

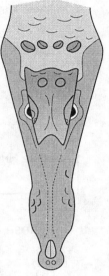

American
Crocodile

American
Alligator

Central America, and as far north as the southern tip of Florida. The American alligator is found only in the southeastern United States. Because it can <u>tolerate</u> cooler waters better than other *crocodilians*, the American alligator can live as far north as North Carolina. It has also been found as far west as Texas.

Even though there are only two *crocodilians* living in the United States, there are many different members of the family living in tropical and subtropical regions of the world. For example, there are the endangered caymans (KAY-mans) of the mighty Amazon river and the famous Nile crocodiles of Egypt.

Here's some advice: "Don't smile at a crocodile," even though it may look like it's smiling at you. A crocodile's bottom fangs stick up outside its upper lip, creating what looks like a grin. (The alligator has these same teeth, but they're hidden under its lip.) Even though a crocodile may look like he's smiling at you, he's not! Luckily, its teeth are large enough to see from a distance. If you should see them, wave a quick good-bye and skip right to "After a while, crocodile!" ❖❖

Sample Comparison Questions

Directions: Answer the following questions. Base your answers on the article "Don't Smile at a Crocodile."

1. Which of the following is one way that alligators and crocodiles are ALIKE?
   - Ⓐ They both can be found in Mississippi.
   - Ⓑ They both can be found in salty ocean waters.
   - Ⓒ They both have powerful tails used for swimming.
   - Ⓓ They both have a narrow snout that comes to a point.

2. Which of the following is one way that alligators are DIFFERENT from crocodiles?
   - Ⓐ Alligators have tough hides.
   - Ⓑ Alligators can live in cooler waters.
   - Ⓒ Alligators have cigar-shaped bodies.
   - Ⓓ Alligators have fangs that stick outside their lip.

3. Which of the following is one way that crocodiles are DIFFERENT from alligators?
   - Ⓐ Crocodiles have sharp teeth.
   - Ⓑ Crocodiles live in fresh water.
   - Ⓒ Crocodiles do not grow more than ten feet long.
   - Ⓓ Crocodiles will attack without being disturbed.

4. Which do you think is more dangerous to humans, the American alligator or the American crocodile? Use details and examples from the article in your answer.

_____

_____

_____

_____

_____

_____

_____

_____

Additional Practice Questions

Directions: Now try answering some other types of questions about the article. You'll learn more about these question types in other lessons of this book.

5. What is the MOST LIKELY reason that daredevil entertainers wrestle alligators rather than crocodiles?
   - Ⓐ Alligators weigh less than crocodiles.
   - Ⓑ Alligators are not an endangered species.
   - Ⓒ Alligators enjoy wrestling more than crocodiles.
   - Ⓓ Alligators are not as fast nor as unfriendly as crocodiles.

6. What does *tolerate* mean?
   - Ⓐ bear
   - Ⓑ find
   - Ⓒ thaw
   - Ⓓ attack

Lesson 8

One Thing Leads to Another

Pretend you have stood a long row of dominoes on end. They are standing very close to each other. What happens if you knock the first domino into the second one? The whole row falls down, one after another.

A story is a lot like that row of dominoes. Something happens first. That event causes the second thing to happen, and so on. Learning about **causes** and their **effects** (results), will help you better understand the things you read.

Cause and Effect Tips

The following tips will help you spot causes and effects in a reading passage. They will also help you answer cause-and-effect questions on the state reading test.

Tip 1 **Put the events in order.**

First, put the events in order. This will help you see the connections between events more clearly. The following passage will help you practice this skill.

Practice Passage

Directions: Read the story "All Wet." Then answer numbers 1 through 5.

All Wet

by Alan Noble

"Mark! Just look at yourself! Why are your new clothes all wet and covered with mud?" My dad seemed very upset.

"Because of a nail, I guess," I said.

"A nail? How could a nail make you wet and dirty?" Dad asked. He was looking very unhappy with me.

"See, it was like this. Today was Phil's birthday party, so I got on my bike to go. As I rode my bike out of the garage, I ran over a nail. The front tire was flat before I got to the end of the driveway."

"And?" my father asked.

"Well, I decided to leave the bike and walk to Phil's. Since I had to walk, I knew I was going to be late. So I thought I'd take a shortcut over the footbridge. When I got to the little creek, the footbridge was closed for repairs. So, I used the stepping stones instead."

"And you slipped," Dad said without a smile.

"Not exactly," I said. "But I did *start* to lose my balance. That's what made me drop Phil's birthday gift into the water."

"Oh, no!" Dad groaned.

"Yeah. And then I had to jump in after it. I finally grabbed it, but the creek bottom was really slick. So I slipped into deeper water."

"So you didn't go to the party?"

"No, Dad. I didn't want to go in these wet clothes. I just dropped off Phil's gift and came home."

"You gave him a wet gift?!" Dad was surprised. "Wasn't the gift ruined?"

"No. It was fine," I said.

"What was it?" he asked.

"Swimming trunks," I said. ❖❖

1. What is the FIRST thing that happens to Mark when he tries to ride his bike to Phil's party?

   _____

That first event causes a long chain of events to happen afterward. Look at the row of dominoes below.

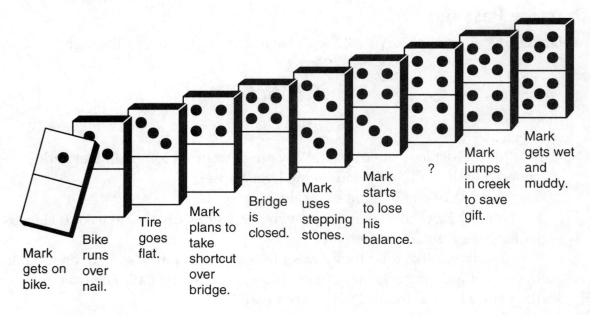

2. What event belongs with domino ?

_____

_____

3. What happens JUST AFTER Mark runs over a nail in the garage?
   - Ⓐ Mark decides to walk.
   - Ⓑ The bicycle tire goes flat.
   - Ⓒ Workmen close the bridge.
   - Ⓓ Mark gets wet and muddy.

 Tip 2 **The event that causes an action usually happens just before the action.**

Most of the time, we can find the cause of an event by looking at what happens just before it.

4. Which event causes Mark to get wet and muddy?
   - Ⓐ He decides to walk through the park.
   - Ⓑ Workmen close the footbridge over the creek.
   - Ⓒ He takes the stepping stones across the creek.
   - Ⓓ He jumps into the creek to save the birthday gift.

Tip 3 **Connect the events in a "because" sentence.**

In the passage, Mark has one problem after another. Each problem is caused by something that happens just before it. We can see the connection between two events if we put them together in a single sentence.

Mark takes the stepping stones across the creek BECAUSE the bridge is closed.

Now it's your turn.

5. Write a "because" sentence that connects two other events from the passage.

_____

BECAUSE _____

_____ .

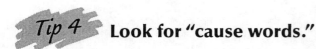   **Look for "cause words."**

The box below shows words that will help you spot causes and effects.

Cause Words
cause
because
so
led to
due to
as a result of

Read the following passage from *The Lemonade Trick* by Scott Corbett. Look for any words that will help you find out "what caused what" to happen.

> Bumps Burton lived next to the vacant lot behind Kerby's house. He was large for his age, and clumsy. He was not very smart in school. Nobody liked him, because he was a big bully. He made a regular hobby of twisting small boys' noses. He considered a day wasted when he didn't twist at least two or three. Occasionally he twisted an ear for good measure.

6. Underline any "cause" words in the passage.

7. Why doesn't anybody like Bumps Burton?

_____

_____

Tip 5 **Look for causes and effects in nonfiction passages, too.**

You will often see connections between events in nonfiction passages. Read the following passage from an article about scallops, a type of shellfish. The article is from *Ranger Rick* (June 1995).

> A scallop's gills are covered with thousands of tiny hairs called cilia (SILL-ee-uh) that are too small to see. These hairs are always quickly waving back and forth. The waving sweeps water into the scallop's shell. The scallop gets oxygen from this water. And floating in the water are tiny plants and animals. They get caught on the cilia and are then swept into the scallop's mouth.

8. How does the movement of the cilia help the scallop?
   Ⓐ The cilia sweep water in to clean the scallop's shell.
   Ⓑ The cilia protect the scallop from dangerous animals.
   Ⓒ The cilia bring in water that contains oxygen and food.
   Ⓓ The cilia keep the scallop's gills warm in cold ocean waters.

Practice Passage

Directions: Read the passage from *Jennifer Murdley's Toad.* Then answer the questions that follow.

from

Jennifer Murdley's Toad

by Bruce Coville

If Jennifer Murdley hadn't been forced to wear her brother's underpants to school, the whole thing might never have happened. But when she walked into the laundry room on the morning of October 13th, she found her father pouring liquid detergent onto a load of clothes that included every pair of underwear she owned.

"Dad!" she screamed. "Wait!"

She was too late. The tub was filling, her underwear was soggy and soapy, and there was no chance of getting any of it dry before she had to leave for school.

"Don't worry," said Mr. Murdley, holding up a stack of neatly folded underpants, "you can wear a pair of these!"

"You have got to be kidding! Those belong to Skippy!"

The conversation that followed wasn't pretty. The bottom line had been that Jennifer *was* going to school, and she *was* going to wear underwear, even if it did belong to her brother.

Although she promised Skippy to keep it a secret, Jennifer confided the embarrassing truth to one person—her best friend, Ellen.

Ellen, not unnaturally, thought it was funny.

So she told Annette.

Annette told Maya.

Maya told Sharra.

And Sharra, as could have been expected, told the world.

By recess every boy in the fifth grade knew Jennifer's secret. They chased her around the playground, chanting, "Jennifer Murdley went to France, wearing her brother's underpants," while Sharra and her friends stood in a circle, giggling and pointing.

As if that weren't bad enough, when Jennifer passed Skippy in the hallway later that day, as her class was leaving art and his was entering, he hissed, "You *die*, creepazoid." ❖❖

Sample Cause-and-Effect Questions

Directions: Answer the following questions. Base your answers on the passage from *Jennifer Murdley's Toad*.

1. Why does Jennifer have to wear her brother's underpants?
   - (A) Her brother's are more neatly folded.
   - (B) Her brother is playing a trick on her.
   - (C) Her father wants to teach her a lesson.
   - (D) Her father put all of hers in the laundry.

2. What is the MAIN cause of Jennifer's trouble at school?
   - (A) Everyone knows her secret.
   - (B) Skippy calls her a creepazoid.
   - (C) Her brother goes to her school.
   - (D) Her friend Ellen is mean to her.

3. Who FIRST causes Jennifer's secret to spread?
   - (A) Maya
   - (B) Jennifer
   - (C) Sharra
   - (D) Skippy

Additional Practice Questions

Directions: Now try answering some other types of questions about the story. You'll learn more about these question types in other lessons of this book.

4. What is Jennifer's MAIN problem?
   - Ⓐ She does not have any friends.
   - Ⓑ Her brother is very angry with her.
   - Ⓒ She has to wear Skippy's underpants.
   - Ⓓ She is late for school on an important day.

5. What does the author mean by "The conversation that followed wasn't pretty"?
   - Ⓐ Skippy's underpants did not look very nice.
   - Ⓑ Mr. Murdley and Jennifer had an argument.
   - Ⓒ Jennifer and her father are not good-looking.
   - Ⓓ Jennifer and her father made ugly faces at each other.

6. What do Ellen and Maya do ALIKE?
   - Ⓐ They both keep Jennifer's secret.
   - Ⓑ They both embarrass Jennifer in art class.
   - Ⓒ They both chase Jennifer around the playground.
   - Ⓓ They both tell someone else about Jennifer's secret.

7. Which of the following was the LAST event to happen before Jennifer's secret spread over the whole school?
   - Ⓐ Maya told Jennifer's secret to Sharra.
   - Ⓑ Jennifer's clothes were in the washer.
   - Ⓒ Jennifer promised Skippy not to tell.
   - Ⓓ Jennifer told her best friend, Ellen.

8. What do you know about Sharra from this story?
   - Ⓐ She is nice to Jennifer.
   - Ⓑ She is friends with Skippy.
   - Ⓒ She doesn't keep secrets.
   - Ⓓ She does not have any friends.

9. How did Skippy feel when he found out that the other kids knew Jennifer was wearing his underpants?
   - Ⓐ pleased that someone else was teasing Jennifer
   - Ⓑ angry that people knew they were his underpants
   - Ⓒ sad because Jennifer's friends didn't keep her secret
   - Ⓓ bored because it seemed a silly thing to tease her about

Hidden Messages

A writer doesn't always come right out and tell the reader everything directly. Sometimes messages are hidden within the text. Your job as a reader is to try to find them.

Practice Passage

Directions: Read the story "The Trouble with Getting Even." It will help you learn about hidden messages.

"Bennnnn-jyyyyyyy," an <u>eerie</u> voice called in the darkness. "Bennnnn-jyyyyyy, where are youuuuuu?" whispered another.

Three-year-old Benjy Booth opened his eyes with a start. What was that? Was someone calling his name? Benjy squinted his eyes to peer through the blackness of his bedroom. A large white shape seemed to be floating in his doorway.

"Bennnnn-jyyyyyy. I'm coming to get youuuuuu," the shape seemed to say.

"Mommy!" Benjy cried. He pulled the covers tightly over his head. He curled up into a tiny ball in the middle of his bed and began to cry loudly.

Within seconds, his parents were at his side. Mom gently tugged at the blankets to uncover the shaking little boy. Dad reached over and turned on the light next to Benjy's bed. It glowed red through the balloon-shaped shade.

"It's all right, Honey," Mom said. "Daddy and Mommy are here. Nothing can hurt you."

Benjy's chest <u>heaved</u> with each sob. His nose ran. Tears streamed down his cheeks. He wiped his eyes and nose with the sleeve of his Spiderman pajamas.

"Tell us what happened, Buddy," Dad said softly.

It was hard for Benjy to stop crying. Between sobs he said, "A g-g-ghost! There was a g-ghost in my room. It tried to get me."

"Sweetheart, there's no ghost in your room. You see, your room is just like it always was. You must have had a bad dream," Mom said.

"What's going on?" a soft voice asked from down the hall. Benjy's big sister Jenny appeared in the doorway, pulling a blue robe over her long white nightgown.

"Yeah, what's up?" It was Karen, Jenny's twin, who peeked into the room from behind her. She and Jenny were dressed identically.

"Benjy had a bad dream," Mom said. "But he's going to be all right now."

Benjy's sobs shook his small body. He peered through wet lashes toward the doorway where moments ago he had seen the ghost. He wasn't quite so scared while Mommy held him. "It wasn't a dream. A g-ghost tried to get me," he said, looking from one girl to the other with tear-filled brown eyes.

Jenny and Karen quickly exchanged glances. They didn't have to say a word—as usual, each twin knew what the other was thinking. This was the little bother who got into everything they owned. He was the terror who broke their toys and colored in their books. And he was the same pain-in-the-neck who had gotten them into trouble yesterday when he ratted on them to their father.

But now, curled up like a baby on Mom's lap, Benjy suddenly seemed innocent and precious. The ten-year-olds shifted their weight from slippered foot to slippered foot. They kept glancing from Benjy to each other and back again.

Mom was too busy cuddling Benjy and cooing comforting words to him to notice what the girls were doing. "It's all right, Honey. Mommy's here," she said.

But Dad didn't miss any of it. "Girls, is there something you'd like to tell us?" he asked. He was looking right at them, and he wasn't smiling. ❖❖

Hidden Messages Tips

 Put together clues from the passage to find hidden messages.

Hidden messages are like mysteries. If you only have one clue, they're hard to figure out. The more clues you have, the easier it is to solve the mystery. In a reading passage, the clues are the details.

Read the following question. (Don't answer it yet.)

What do the twins think about their little brother MOST of the time?

Now answer numbers 1 through 3.

1. Go back to the story and draw a box around the paragraph that best tells what the girls think about Benjy MOST of the time.

2. Write three details from the paragraph that tell why the girls think the way they do about Benjy?

   a. _____

   _____

   b. _____

   _____

   c. _____

   _____

3. What do the twins think about their little brother MOST of the time?
   Ⓐ He acts like a baby.
   Ⓑ He is a bit of a pest.
   Ⓒ He is sweet and cuddly.
   Ⓓ He is innocent and precious.

![Tip 2] **Draw conclusions based on what you have read.**

Sometimes the clues in a passage are so clearly connected that you can't miss them. Other times, you may need to make what's called an "educated guess."

When you make an educated guess, you don't have all the information you need. You have to think carefully about what you *do* know before you make a decision. An educated guess is not a wild guess, but it's still a guess.

Make an educated guess to answer the next question.

4. What was the ghost that Benjy saw?

_____

_____

5. Underline details in the story that support your answer to number 4.

Sample "Hidden Messages" Questions

Directions: Answer the following questions. Base your answers on the story "The Trouble with Getting Even."

1. Why isn't Dad smiling when he looks at the girls at the end of the passage?
   Ⓐ He is angry at the girls.
   Ⓑ He is too tired to smile.
   Ⓒ He is frightened for Benjy.
   Ⓓ He doesn't know what has happened.

2. What does the fact that the girls "shifted from slippered foot to slippered foot" MOST LIKELY tell us about them?
   Ⓐ They were cold.
   Ⓑ They were very tired.
   Ⓒ They were feeling guilty.
   Ⓓ They wanted to sit down.

Additional Practice Questions

Directions: Now try answering some other types of questions about the story. You'll learn more about these question types in other lessons of this book.

3. What does *eerie* mean?
   - Ⓐ tired and sleepy
   - Ⓑ mysterious and scary
   - Ⓒ pleasant and cheerful
   - Ⓓ funny and entertaining

4. What does *heaved* mean?
   - Ⓐ stayed very still
   - Ⓑ stopped hurting
   - Ⓒ lifted up suddenly
   - Ⓓ grew smaller and smaller

5. What is MOST LIKELY to happen next in the story?
   - Ⓐ Dad will scare Benjy.
   - Ⓑ The twins will get mad at Benjy.
   - Ⓒ Another ghost will frighten Benjy.
   - Ⓓ The twins will tell Dad something.

6. What is the author's purpose for writing "The Trouble with Getting Even"?
   - Ⓐ to persuade the reader not to believe in ghosts
   - Ⓑ to entertain the reader with an interesting story
   - Ⓒ to teach the reader important facts about ghosts
   - Ⓓ to show the reader how to get along with brothers and sisters

7. In what ways are Jenny and Karen ALIKE? Use details from the story to explain your answer.

   _____

   _____

   _____

   _____

Getting to Know the Author

Lesson 10

The Writer Behind the Writing

You can tell a lot about a writer from the things he or she has written. By reading closely, you can learn the author's purpose, message, and attitude toward the topic.

Practice Passage

Directions: Read the following script for a TV commercial. It will help you understand the lesson.

by Edgar Cranston

The camera zooms in on a boy (NELSON) and a girl (DESSE) sitting at their kitchen table. The boy has a heaping bowl of cereal. The girl's bowl is empty. She is holding an empty box of Power Pack cereal upside down over her bowl. She shakes it, but nothing comes out.

DESSE: Nelson, you ate the rest of the Power Pack cereal! *She gives him an angry look.* Nothing else tastes as good as Power Pack.

NELSON: You're right. Power Pack is the best-tasting cereal there is. And Power Pack makes me feel really strong—like I'm the most powerful person in the world!

He suddenly changes into an adult professional wrestler, but his voice stays the same.

Power Pack gives me vitamins and minerals that make me strong.

DESSE: Well, I need vitamins and minerals, too. Power Pack helps me be a champion gymnast. Besides, Power Pack tastes great! If I only had some now . . . *Her voice trails off.*

MOM enters carrying a bag of groceries. She pulls out a new box of Power Pack.

DESSE: Great, Mom! You bought more Power Pack!

DESSE pours a bowl of cereal and adds milk. She takes a bite and turns into an adult Olympic gymnast with four gold medals hanging around her neck.

MOM (smiling): Why, Power Pack has made such a change in you, I hardly recognize my own children anymore!

ANNOUNCER: Why not make Power Pack part of your morning? It's a part of this complete nutritious breakfast.

Camera shows orange juice, toast, bacon, and a glass of milk along with Power Pack cereal.

Camera shows DESSE, NELSON, and MOM all sitting down eating Power Pack cereal with big smiles on their faces. ❖❖

Author's Purpose Tips

Most of the time a writer won't tell the reader directly why he or she wrote a story or article. By paying close attention, however, you can figure out the author's purpose. Here are a few tips to help you.

 Tip 1 **Look for clues that tell why the author wrote the passage.**

Fiction passages are usually written to **entertain** readers. If the writer wants to frighten the reader, the story will be scary. If the writer wants to make the reader laugh, the story will be funny.

Nonfiction passages may be written for several purposes. Sometimes the author wants to **teach** or **inform** the reader about a topic. These passages are usually filled with facts and little or no opinion. If there are two or more sides to an issue, the writer presents them all as being of equal value.

Sometimes an author wants to **persuade** or **convince** the reader to take a certain view. These passages are usually filled with opinions. If there are two or more sides to an issue, the writer presents one of them as being the best.

1. What is the main reason the author wrote "Power Up with Power Pack!"?
   - Ⓐ to teach viewers how to prepare healthy meals
   - Ⓑ to persuade viewers to buy a certain brand of cereal
   - Ⓒ to tell viewers about children who are great athletes
   - Ⓓ to persuade viewers not to skip breakfast in the mornings

Tip 2 **Pay attention to the author's attitude.**

Attitude is the way a person feels about something. We each have different attitudes about different things. For example, you might have a positive attitude toward double-chocolate-crunch ice cream. On the other hand, you might have a negative attitude toward liver and pickle sandwiches.

Authors have attitudes, too—attitudes about the things they are writing about. One clue to the author's attitude is the **tone** he or she uses. The tone of an author's writing is much like the tone someone uses when speaking.

For example, you can probably tell from the tone of your parent's voice whether he or she is happy with something you have done. You can also tell when he or she is not so happy.

The tone of a reading passage is generally either positive, negative, or neutral.

- A **positive** tone might show happiness, hope, joy, excitement, pride, or any number of other "good" feelings.

- A **negative** tone might show sorrow, shame, fear, anger, or other "bad" feelings.

- A **neutral** tone doesn't show strong feelings one way or the other.

Practice Passage

Directions: Read the following letter. Then answer numbers 1 through 5. The letter was written in response to a newspaper article titled "Should Students Use Calculators?"

Letter to the Editor

Dear Editor,

I think we should be allowed to use calculators in school. Calculators are used every day all over the world. Like computers, they are important tools we should learn how to use.

Some people say calculators would keep us from learning how to do things like addition and multiplication in our minds. Here is my idea: Allow us to use calculators only on tests. We would get plenty of practice doing math problems the long way on our homework. On test day, we would spend less time writing to figure out the answers. The time we save could be spent answering even more problems.

Because we would write less, our papers wouldn't be as messy. Teachers could grade them faster and easier. We would use less paper on tests, and that's good for the environment. Also, my hand would be a lot less tired at the end of the day.

I hope your readers will think about these ideas.

Sincerely,

Coy Scott

Coy Scott

2. What is the author's tone in this letter? Circle one.

   Positive   Negative   Neutral

3. What is the author's attitude toward the idea of using calculators in school?
   - Ⓐ joking
   - Ⓑ approving
   - Ⓒ mistrustful
   - Ⓓ uninterested

4. Why did the author write this letter?
   - Ⓐ to tell how to use calculators to solve problems
   - Ⓑ to persuade people to use calculators more often
   - Ⓒ to entertain with a funny story about taking tests
   - Ⓓ to persuade people that students should use calculators

5. How do you know?

   _____

   _____

   _____

6. Do you agree or disagree with the author's ideas? Why? Use details from the letter in your answer.

   _____

   _____

   _____

   _____

   _____

   _____

   _____

Tip 3 **Look for the author's message.**

The author's message will be the main idea of the passage. Ask yourself, "What idea is the author trying to get across?

Tip 4 **Determine whether a statement is FACT or OPINION.**

A **fact** statement can be checked. Fact statements use words with meanings everyone can agree on.

Examples of Fact Words			
red	twenty	round	Canadian
empty	open	plastic	metal
broken	first place	polka-dotted	square

If your friend Mika says, "My guinea pig Bruiser weighs less than a pound," she's making a statement of fact. You can check to see if her statement is correct by putting Bruiser on a scale.

Of course, Mika might be wrong. Bruiser might weigh more or less than a pound. Even so, Mika's statement isn't her opinion. We know she made a statement of fact because it can be checked out.

An **opinion** statement cannot be checked. Opinion statements often use words that mean different things to different people.

Examples of Opinion Words	
lovely—ugly	cruel—kind
frightening—enjoyable	delicious—disgusting
wonderful—horrible	worst—best
a lot—a little	cool—gross

If Mika says that Bruiser is "the sweetest little piggy you could ever hope to meet," she's stating her opinion. She may think he's the sweetest; you may think he's a monster. Some people will agree with Mika. Some will agree with you. Her opinion about Bruiser can't be checked out.

Practice Activity

Directions: Read the following sentences. Put an "**F**" in front of each **Fact** statement. Put an "**O**" in front of each **Opinion** statement.

_____ 7. Island Beach State Park is the most beautiful park in the entire country.

_____ 8. The first scene in the movie *The Karate Kid* takes place in Newark, New Jersey.

_____ 9. The New Jersey Devils hockey team won the Stanley Cup in 1994.

_____ 10. R. L. Stine writes really scary books.

_____ 11. When I type on a computer keyboard, my fingers make a sound like chickens dancing on the roof.

_____ 12. Every summer, my family takes a vacation in Atlantic City.

_____ 13. Apollo 11, the first manned moon mission, lifted off on July 16, 1969.

_____ 14. The New Jersey Nets are the best basketball team ever!

_____ 15. The public library in Trenton has every book in the Boxcar Children series.

_____ 16. The movie we should watch is *Anastasia*.

 Tip 5 **Compare the author's ideas to those of another author.**

Don't take one author's word for it. Find out what someone else has to say. Then decide what you think.

Practice Passage

Directions: Read the "Letters to the Editor." Then answer the questions that follow.

City News

Letters to the Editor

Passage 1

Dear Editor,

I read your article in last Sunday's *Gazette* titled "Pennies: Are They Worth It?" I, too, believe that we should do away with pennies. Many people do not like to carry pennies because they weigh down pockets and purses. Many families have jars full of pennies just sitting around. They are worth so little that most people will not stoop to pick one up. The U.S. Mint has to keep making pennies because so many people do not spend them.

It is true that if we eliminated the penny, our money system would need to change. Merchants would have to set prices differently, or prices would need to be rounded to the nearest nickel. But we would not be the only country to try this. Other countries have also changed their money systems. The British have eliminated their farthing, which was much like our penny. And our own country has made similar changes in the past. In the 1800s, our government issued half-cent, two-cent, and three-cent coins.

Because American life is changing and improving a great deal, our money system could stand some improvement as well.

Sincerely,

Albert E. Finestine

Albert E. Finestine

Passage 2

To the Editor,

   In last Sunday's article, "Pennies: Are They Worth It?" the author brings up a number of interesting points about the "need" to get rid of pennies. However, I must disagree with most of them. Pennies are an important part of our money system and should not be removed.

   The article suggests that if pennies were no longer used, prices would need to be rounded to the nearest nickel. Prices would most likely be rounded up. Imagine adding between one and four cents to every single item you buy. (How many items do you buy each time you go to the grocery store?) The money would add up pretty fast.

   If it were decided that pennies were no longer to be used, how long after this decision would they be accepted? Would they become useless immediately, or would there be some period during which people could get rid of them? And what would happen to the pennies that people have? Could they be cashed in at banks? Or would people be stuck with piles of worthless copper-coated zinc? All this seems like a lot of trouble to go through just to get rid of something that we should be keeping.

   My final reason for not wanting to get rid of pennies is purely a sentimental one, but it is one I think many people share. You've heard the saying, "Find a penny, pick it up. All day long you'll have good luck." Everyone feels in need of a little bit of luck once in a while. If pennies are done away with, what exactly would you have us pick up?

Yours truly,

Phillis Jeter

Phillis Jeter

Sample Author Questions

Directions: Answer the following questions. Base your answers on "Letters to the Editor."

  1. What is Mr. Finestine's purpose for writing Passage 1?
     - Ⓐ to teach people about the history of pennies
     - Ⓑ to disagree with the article "Pennies: Are They Worth It?"
     - Ⓒ to convince readers that the penny should be done away with
     - Ⓓ to inform people that shopping would be more expensive without pennies

2. Which of the following statements from Passage 1 is an OPINION?

   Ⓐ "In the 1800s, our government issued half-cent, two-cent, and three-cent coins."

   Ⓑ "Other countries have also changed their money systems."

   Ⓒ "I read your article in last Sunday's *Gazette* titled 'Pennies: Are They Worth It?' "

   Ⓓ "Because American life is changing and improving a great deal, our money system could stand some improvement as well."

3. Why does Phillis Jeter include the last paragraph in Passage 2?

   Ⓐ She is feeling very lucky after writing her letter.

   Ⓑ She wants to argue that all pennies bring people luck.

   Ⓒ She thinks that whether pennies are done away with is totally based on luck.

   Ⓓ She wants to show that to some people pennies are be worth more than just one cent.

4. Which of the following statements from Passage 2 is a FACT?

   Ⓐ "Pennies are an important part of our money system and should not be removed."

   Ⓑ "The article suggests that if pennies were no longer used, prices would need to be rounded to the nearest nickel."

   Ⓒ "All this seems like a lot of trouble to go through just to get rid of something that we should be keeping."

   Ⓓ "Everyone feels in need of a little bit of luck once in a while."

5. With which passage would the author of "Pennies: Are They Worth It?" most likely agree?

   Ⓐ Passage 1

   Ⓑ Passage 2

   Ⓒ both passages

   Ⓓ neither passage

6. On which of the following points do Albert Finestine and Phillis Jeter agree?

   Ⓐ Most people think that pennies are worthless.

   Ⓑ People enjoy stooping to pick up a penny for good luck.

   Ⓒ Doing away with pennies would require other changes in our money system.

   Ⓓ Our country should follow the lead of Britain in changing our money system.

Additional Practice Question

Directions: Now try answering another type of question about the article. You'll learn more about this question type in Lesson 14.

7. What is your opinion about the future of pennies? Do you think they should remain in our money system? Or should they be done away with? Use details from the "Letters to the Editor" to support your answer.

_____

_____

_____

_____

_____

_____

_____

_____

_____

Lesson 11

The Writer's Bag of Tricks

Writers have many ways to get their ideas across. In this lesson, you will learn about a few of the methods writers use.

Writer's Methods

 **Notice how the writer compares things.**

Similes compare two things by using the words *like* or *as*.

> My Aunt Roberta always says, "Eliza, you're growing <u>like</u> a weed."

Metaphors compare two things by say that one thing *is* another.

> America <u>is</u> a melting pot, blending people from many cultures.

Practice Passage

Directions: Read the poem "The Moon's the North Wind's Cooky." Then answer numbers 1 through 3.

The Moon's the North Wind's Cooky

by Vachel Lindsay

The Moon's the North Wind's cooky.*
He bites it, day by day,
Until there's but a rim of scraps
That crumble all away.
The South Wind is a baker.
He kneads clouds in his den,
And bakes a crisp new moon *that . . greedy*
North . . Wind . . eats . . again!

*****cooky:** cookie

1. Find two lines in the poem that contain metaphors. Underline them.

2. According to the poet, how is the moon like a cookie?

   _____

   _____

   _____

   _____

   _____

3. What is this poem actually describing?
   - Ⓐ the habits of the man in the moon
   - Ⓑ the daily work of a baker in a bakery
   - Ⓒ a greedy man who eats someone else's cookies
   - Ⓓ the cycles of the moon as it travels around Earth

 Notice the way a writer makes things seem real.

Personification is when the author gives an animal or object human qualities, making it "person-like."

    Dad screamed as he watched the copying machine eat page after page. There went the report he had worked on for weeks.

Copying machines may tear and crumple paper, but they don't really "eat" it.

4. Read the following lines from the poem "Water" by child poet Hilda Conkling. Underline any words in the poem that show personification.

   The world turns softly
   Not to spill its lakes and rivers.
   The water is held in its arms

Authors also use **sensory words** to create images. Sensory words tell how something looks, tastes, feels, sounds, or smells.

5. Underline the sensory words in the paragraph below.

> The spicy scent of Marvin's mystery soup filled the house. I peeked into the kitchen and saw the brown liquid oozing from under the lid, sizzling as it slid down the sides of the pot and hit the burner. I walked over and lifted the lid, feeling the steam warm my face. I looked inside, not believing what I saw—floating bits of red and green, and every now and then, something that looked like an eyeball.

Tip 3 **Notice sounds the writer uses.**

One way a poet creates the "music" of a poem is with the **rhythm** the words make. Rhythm in a poem is like the "beat" in a song.

Read the following lines from a poem by Robert Browning. Then answer number 6.

> I sprang to the stirrup, and Joris, and he;
> I galloped, Dirck galloped, we galloped all three;

6. Read the lines again several times. Try reading them aloud. Notice the rhythm the words make. What does this rhythm remind you of? Why did the poet write these lines in this way?

_____

_____

_____

Sometimes the first thing we notice about a poem is whether or not the lines **rhyme**. Rhyme is another way a poet makes the "music" of a poem. Not all poems rhyme, but many do.

Alliteration uses a series of words that start with the same consonant sound. "Peter Piper picked a peck of pickled peppers" is an example of alliteration.

Read the following lines from the poem "My Heart's in the Highlands" by Robert Burns.

> My heart's in the Highlands, my heart is not here;
> My heart's in the Highlands a-chasing the deer.

7. Circle any words that show use of rhyme.

8. Underline any words that show use of alliteration.

 Notice how the writer stresses ideas.

Authors often use **repetition** to stress meaning. An example is given below.

Practice Passage

Directions: Read the poem "Some One." Then answer numbers 9 and 10.

Some One

by Walter de la Mare

Some one came knocking,
  At my wee, small door;
Some one came knocking;
  I'm sure—sure—sure;
I listened, I opened,
  I looked to left and right,
But nought there was a-stirring
  In the still dark night;
Only the busy beetle
  Tap-tapping in the wall,
Only from the forest
  The screech-owl's call,
Only the cricket whistling
  While the dew drops fall,
So I know not who came knocking,
  At all, at all, at all.

9. What words are repeated in the poem?

_____

_____

_____

10. This repetition reminds the reader of what sound?
    Ⓐ the sound of a door opening
    Ⓑ the sound of a cricket whistling
    Ⓒ the sound of knocking on a door
    Ⓓ the sound of a screech owl's call

Exaggeration is also used to stress meaning. An author may use exaggeration to make a point or simply to get a laugh. Another word for exaggeration is **hyperbole** (Hi-PER-ba-lee).

This soup is thicker than the mud at the bottom of a Pine Barrens swamp.

All the chocolate in Hershey, Pennsylvania, wouldn't be enough for Charlotte.

 Look for other methods the author uses.

Authors often use such special methods to capture your interest and keep you turning the pages. Two methods authors often use are **foreshadowing** and **flashbacks**.

Foreshadowing is when the author gives hints that something will happen later in the story.

Practice Passage

Directions: Read the following passage from *Fright in the Forest*. It will help you learn about foreshadowing.

from

Fright in the Forest

by Kay Kryptson

"If we played one more game, I could beat you," Scott said. He and his cousin Bridgette had been playing Chinese checkers for three hours straight. Bridgette had won every time. "But I've got to get home or Mom's gonna have a cow."

"Yeah, you were supposed to be home an hour ago," Bridgette said. "Now you'll have to walk in the dark—without a flashlight."

Scott and Bridgette lived on opposite sides of a small wooded area. Pickens Forest, it was called. Scott didn't think it was big enough to be called a forest. The trees certainly were thick enough, though. And at night, it could be pretty dark in there.

A narrow trail wound through the woods between their houses. Scott usually had a flashlight to help him find his way down the trail, but this time he had forgotten it.

So what, he thought. *I've been down that trail a zillion times.*

"See ya tomorrow at school," Scott said as he walked out the back door of Bridgette's house.

"Yeah. That is, *if* you make it home tonight," Bridgette teased.

The field in back of the house glowed with the bluish light of a full moon. The tall grass swayed softly as Scott walked toward the trail entrance at the edge of the woods. But as he got closer, the moon slipped behind a heavy cloud. Suddenly everything was pitch black, and where the trail disappeared into the woods, it was even pitch blacker.

No big deal, Scott told himself. *Nothing's in those woods but squirrels and raccoons.*

At least he *hoped* that was all. Unfortunately, he was wrong.

As he walked down the trail, Scott took his mind off the eerie shadows by thinking about his checkers game. Bridgette was good, no doubt about it. But he thought he could eventually beat her. *I'll challenge her to another game tomorrow,* he said to himself. ❖❖

11. What do you think will happen next in the story?

_____

_____

_____

12. How do you know?

_____

_____

_____

13. Go back to the passage and mark any examples of foreshadowing.

An author may use **flashbacks** to tell about events that happened earlier. The author interrupts the story, writes about a scene in the past, and then comes back to the story.

Let's return to *Fright in the Forest*. As the story continues, Scott begins to hear eerie sounds as he walks along the trail—sounds that aren't quite like anything he's heard before. Then we come to this scene:

> Scott decided to pick up the pace a bit. For some reason, he started thinking about how he had scared his little brother that morning.
> "You'd better not go in my room," he had said to Logan. "A troll lives in there."
> "Scott, you'd better stop scaring Logan," Bridgette scolded. "You got in big trouble the last time your mom caught you."
> "But it's the only way to keep him out of my room!" Scott answered.
> Scott loved his little brother. He was a cute little redhead with pudgy cheeks and a big I-trust-you smile. But the older he got, the more he got into Scott's things. And a guy can have a lot of things by the time he's nine years old.
> Now Scott felt more scared than he had ever been in his life. He thought, *If I ever make it home, Logan can play in my room anytime he wants.*

14. Use your pencil to mark where the flashback begins in the passage. Then mark where the flashback ends.

Practice Passage

Directions: Read the poem "The Frogs of Tarrydiddle Pond." Then answer the questions that follow.

The Frogs of Tarrydiddle Pond

by Mickey Toom

The frogs of Tarrydiddle Pond
Went swimming in cold weather
Until their skin
Grew green and thin
And wrinkled like old leather.

Those little Tarrydiddle frogs
Blew bubbles when <u>corrected</u>
And laughed away
The summer day,
Despite what Mom expected.

The frogs of Tarrydiddle pond
Ignored their mother's hushes
And sang their song
The whole night long
Amid the swaying rushes.

And now those Tarrydiddle frogs
Who laughed with glee and joked
Have caught the flu.
They've all turned blue
And wheezed
      —and coughed
           —and croaked!

Sample Writer's Methods Questions

Directions: Answer the following questions. Base your answers on the poem "The Frogs of Tarrydiddle Pond."

1. Read the following lines from the poem.

    Until their skin
    Grew green and thin
    And wrinkled like old leather.

    These lines use which of the following?
    Ⓐ simile
    Ⓑ metaphor
    Ⓒ repetition
    Ⓓ personification

2. Which lines rhyme?
    Ⓐ "Those little Tarrydiddle frogs/Blew bubbles when corrected"
    Ⓑ "And laughed away/The summer day,"
    Ⓒ "Despite what Mom expected/The frogs of Tarrydiddle pond"
    Ⓓ "Ignored their mother's hushes/And sang their song"

3. Which of the following lines uses sensory words?
    Ⓐ "The whole night long"
    Ⓑ "And now those Tarrydiddle frogs"
    Ⓒ "Have caught the flu"
    Ⓓ "They've all turned blue"

4. Read the following lines from the poem.

    Those little Tarrydiddle frogs
    . . . laughed away
    The summer day,

    These lines use which of the following?
    Ⓐ simile
    Ⓑ metaphor
    Ⓒ repetition
    Ⓓ personification

Additional Practice Questions

Directions: Now try answering some other types of questions about the poem. You'll learn more about these question types in other lessons of this book.

5. What does *corrected* mean in the second stanza?
   Ⓐ teased
   Ⓑ soothed
   Ⓒ scolded
   Ⓓ repaired

6. This poem might be found in which of the following books?
   Ⓐ *Animal Poems to Make You Laugh*
   Ⓑ *New Jersey's Ponds, Lakes, and Streams*
   Ⓒ *Types of Frogs and Where to Find Them*
   Ⓓ *Famous Plays from Children's Fairy Tales*

7. What does the mother in the poem want the frogs to do?
   Ⓐ learn to sing better
   Ⓑ stop having so much fun
   Ⓒ take better care of their skin
   Ⓓ be quiet and come out of the cold water

8. What is the poet's message in this poem? Use details and examples from the poem in your answer.

   _____

   _____

   _____

   _____

   _____

Reading Beyond the Lines

UNIT 4

Read All About It

The best way to practice reading is by choosing books you find interesting. Books have been written about almost every topic you can imagine. Listening to music, playing outdoors, spending time with friends—whatever you enjoy, there is probably a book about it.

You also can read to learn new things. You might need to write a report for school. Or maybe you want to learn more about the place your family is going on vacation this summer.

Whatever your purpose, the library is the place to start. Libraries contain books and other reference sources that will tell you about almost anything.

Tips for Choosing Your Own Reading Materials

In this lesson, you will learn a few tips to help you choose reading materials on your own.

 Think about what interests you.

1. In the space below, list some of the things you are interested in. Be as specific as possible. A few general topics are shown to help you get started. You may list things about which you know a lot or only a little.

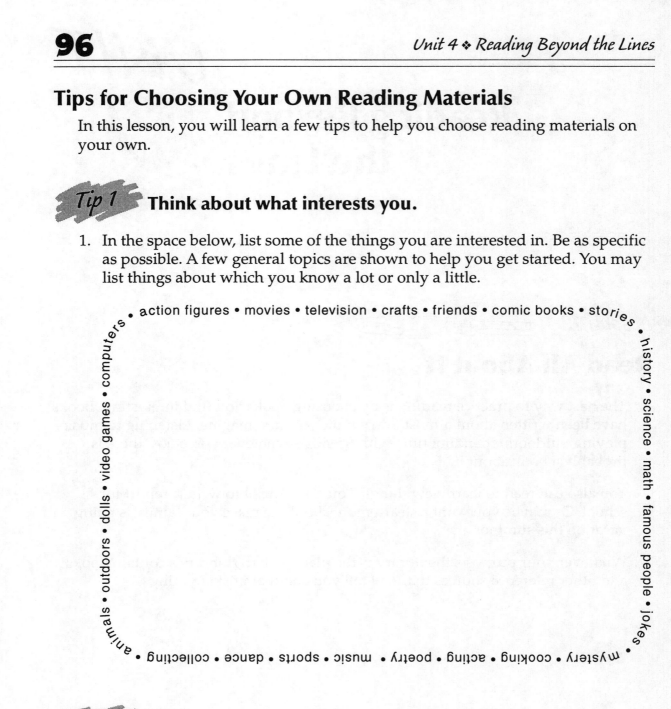

action figures • movies • television • crafts • friends • comic books • stories • history • science • math • famous people • jokes • mystery • cooking • acting • poetry • music • sports • dance • collecting • animals • outdoors • dolls • video games • computers

 Decide what general subject area your topic fits into.

Perhaps you are interested in learning more about your pet boa constrictor. You might have a difficult time finding a book about only boa constrictors. But you can probably find many books about a broader topic: snakes.

2. Look at the list of topics below. Draw a line to match each topic on the left with its category on the right.

Bill Clinton   recording artists

a leaky kitchen faucet   royalty

Walt Disney's *Hercules*   health and fitness

Bruce Springsteen   U.S. Presidents

Queen Elizabeth II   plumbing

baseball card collecting   movies

exercise tips   hobbies

3. Look at the list of topics you wrote under number 1.

a. Choose one topic that you would like to learn more about. Circle it.

b. What general subject area does your topic fit into?

 Think about the types of books available.

Whatever you're interested in, many different types of books have probably been written on the subject. Most books fall into one of the following groups.

Fiction books contain made-up stories. There are many kinds of fiction stories, such as fantasy, mystery, horror, humor, adventure, science fiction, historical fiction, realistic stories, sports stories . . . The list goes on and on!

Short stories are only a few pages long. **Novels** are much longer stories, usually a hundred pages or more. Novels are usually divided into chapters.

Poetry books contain poems. There are many kinds of poems. Some poems are long, some are short. Some poems rhyme, others don't. A poem might tell a story, or it might be total nonsense.

Poems have one thing in common: They express feelings and ideas in as few words as possible. In a poem, every word counts. Poems also tend to be written in lines and stanzas rather than in sentences and paragraphs.

Drama books contain plays. Whenever you watch television or a movie, you are watching a play. Before the story was put on film, someone wrote it down. The playwright (or, in the case of movies and television, the screenwriter) had to write the story in such a way that the actors could easily tell which lines to speak. The actors also need to know where and how to move on the stage. (These are called stage directions.)

Here are a few lines from *Charlie and the Chocolate Factory* by Roald Dahl. This story was adapted into a play by Richard R. George.

VERUCA SALT: (*Screaming as she looks over the edge of the river*) Look! Look over there! What is it? He's moving! He's walking! Why, it's a little person! It's a little man! Down there behind one of the pipes!

(*Everyone rushes to the edge of the river to get a better look*)

CHARLIE: She's right, Grandpa! It *is* a little man! Can you see him?

GRANDPA JOE: I see him Charlie! . . .

WILLY WONKA: . . . They are the Oompa-Loompas!

Nonfiction books also come in many varieties. The one thing they have in common is that they give "real-life" information, not made-up stories. You might find a "how-to" book that gives tips for improving your skateboarding skills. Or you might find a book that tells the history of skateboarding. You might even read a biography of famous skateboarder Tommy "Toothless" Goggins.

4. Look back at the topic you chose under number 3. What type of book would you most like to read about your topic? Circle one of the following:

Fiction

Poetry

Drama

Nonfiction

Practice Activity 1

5. Draw a line matching each type of writing on the left to its definition on the right.

biography

a book about someone's life

drama

informal nonfiction writing on a single topic; expresses the personality of the author; usually short

fable

a book of poems

folktale

a book that tells about important events in the past; not a made-up story

historical fiction

a book that tells how to do something

history

a fantastic made-up story about scientific possibilities, such as space travel to other planets; often set in the future

instruction/"how to"

a play

a realistic made-up story set in the past

mystery

a story that gives clues that are used to discover how or why something happened

poetry

a story using animals with human qualities to illustrate a moral or lesson

science fiction

a traditional story passed down from generation to generation by word of mouth

essay

Practice Activity 2

Directions: On the lines provided, write the type of book each title represents. Choose from:

- biography
- folktale
- history
- instruction/"how to"
- mystery
- poetry
- science fiction
- sports fiction

6. *The Missing Gator of Gumbo Limbo* by Jean Craighead George

_____

7. *Martin Luther King: The Peaceful Warrior* by Ed Clayton

_____

8. *Skateboards: How to Make Them, How to Ride Them* by Glenn and Eve Bunting

_____

9. *Yeh-Shen: A Cinderella Story from China* by Louie Ai-Ling

_____

10. *Aliens Ate My Homework* by Bruce Coville

_____

11. *Dancing Teepees: Poems of American Indian Youth* by Virginia Driving Hawk Sneve

_____

12. *Look Who's Playing First Base* by Matt Christopher

_____

13. *Growing Up in America: 1830–1860* by Velyn Toynton

_____

In the first part of this lesson, you learned about the many types of books available. The following tips will teach you about other types of resources. These resources can be found in your school library or in the public library in your town.

Tip 4 · A dictionary tells about words and their meanings.

A **dictionary** is a book filled with many of the words that make up a language. All the words are listed in alphabetical order from A to Z. A dictionary doesn't change much from year to year, although a few new words are added from time to time.

An American English dictionary contains the English words spoken in the United States. A Spanish/English dictionary contains Spanish words and their English definitions. Use a dictionary to find out the following:

- correct spellings
- definitions
- parts of speech (like "verb," "noun," or "adjective")

Tip 5 · An atlas is a book of maps.

An **atlas** is filled with maps. There are many different kinds of atlases. Some show maps of a certain part of the world, such as the *Atlas of North America*. Others contain maps of the entire world. If your family takes a car trip across the country, the driver might use the *United States Road Atlas*.

The land features shown in atlases don't change from year to year. But the borders of nations might change as governments take over new territory or give up control of an area. Names of cities sometimes change, too.

Use an atlas to find information about the following:

- borders and boundaries between counties, states, and nations
- bodies of water, such as oceans, rivers, and lakes
- land formations, such as continents, mountain ranges, deserts, and plains
- populations of counties, cities, and nations

An encyclopedia tells a little bit about almost everything.

An **encyclopedia** contains facts and explanations about a wide variety of subjects. The topics are arranged in alphabetical order. Some encyclopedias, like the *World Book Encyclopedia*, contain information about almost every subject you could think of. A large set of encyclopedias might look something like this.

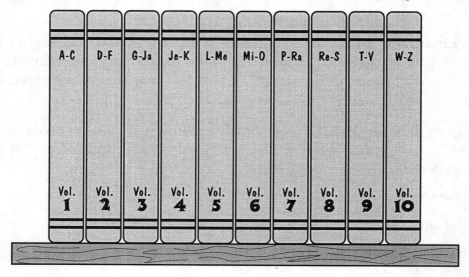

Other encyclopedias, such as the *Encyclopedia of Winter Sports* or the *Encyclopedia of American Artists*, discuss only certain kinds of topics.

Use an encyclopedia when you need more information than a dictionary or atlas can give you.

 An almanac is a book of facts.

An **almanac** contains facts about all kinds of topics. It is published every year, so the information is fairly up-to-date. Many of the facts may change from year to year.

Use an almanac to find lists of facts, such as these:

- the number of students enrolled in school in New Jersey
- the names of all the athletes in the National Baseball Hall of Fame
- the names of crew members aboard each space shuttle mission since 1981
- a list of the 36 fastest animals on Earth, with their speeds in miles per hour
- a list of the year's top 20 best-selling children's books

Magazines contain articles about all kinds of things.

Magazines are published on all kinds of subjects. Some magazines have articles about types of hobbies: listening to music, drawing and painting, cooking, or building and repairing things. Other magazines, such as *Sports Illustrated for Kids*, have articles about sports. Some magazines even have stories in them, such as the ones in *American Girl* and *Boys' Life*.

Magazine articles tend to be more up-to-date than encyclopedia articles. Magazines like *Newsweek* and *Time* contain information about important events in the news. But magazines come out less often than newspapers do. They usually have less information about day-to-day events than newspapers.

 Newspapers tell about important day-to-day events.

Newspapers are usually printed daily. They have articles about important day-to-day events. If you want to learn about what the president of the United States said yesterday in a speech, you would probably look in a newspaper.

 A directory is a list.

A **directory** is a list of information, usually on a single topic. One directory you have probably used is the telephone directory. It lists the names and phone numbers of people in your area.

Practice Activity 3

Directions: Draw a line to match the title on the left with the type of reference on the right.

14. almanac   *Computer Terms and Their Meanings*

15. atlas   *Maps of the Western Hemisphere*

16. dictionary   *National Geographic World*

17. directory   *The 1998 Book of Facts*

18. encyclopedia   *The Model Railroad Encyclopedia*

19. magazine   *The New York Times*

20. newspaper   *U.S. ZIP Codes*

Practice Activity 4

Directions: Write the type of reference needed for each item. Choose from:

- almanac   • atlas   • dictionary   • directory
- encyclopedia   • magazine   • newspaper

21. To find the meaning of the word "dewlap," the best place to look would be a(an):

_____

22. To read about last night's Seton Hall basketball game, the best place to look would be a(an):

_____

23. To find a map of Canada, the best place to look would be a(an):

_____

24. To read a new short story written for kids, the best place to look would be a(an):

   _____

25. To find an article that has general information about the Gulf of Mexico, the best place to look would be a(an):

   _____

26. To find out how many endangered species are in New Jersey, the best place to look would be a(an):

   _____

27. To find the name and phone number of a veterinarian in your area, the best place to look would be a(an):

   _____

 Tip 11 **Learn to use visual resources.**

Some articles will give visual resources to help you understand the topic.

For example, an article about the Hackensack River might include a **map** of the river.

An article about an invention—a gadget that turns tap water into a fizzy cola— might include an **illustration** showing how the invention works.

An article about Mir, the Russian space station, might contain **photos** of astronauts performing experiments in the station.

An article about field trips might include a **chart** listing the 20 most popular field trip destinations in New Jersey. The chart might also include the number of students who visit each year, entrance fees, and phone numbers to call for more information.

When using visual resources, follow these steps.

Step 1: Look for a title.

The title, if there is one, will tell what the visual information is mostly about.

Step 2: Read the text carefully.

Visual resources often come with captions or other text that give important information. Read this text carefully.

Step 3: Think about how the information relates to the article.

Think about how the visual information relates to the rest of the article. Does it give new information? Does it expand on information already given?

Practice Passage

Directions: Read the article "The Wizard of Menlo Park." Then answer the questions that follow.

The Wizard of Menlo Park

by Hugh Moser

Have you seen a movie lately? Played a CD? Turned on a light? If the answer is "yes," you should thank Thomas Edison.

Edison was born in Ohio, but he lived most of his life in New Jersey, first in Newark and later in Menlo Park. He became interested in science and business at a young age, and started inventing when he was 21 years old.

Edison's first famous invention worked with sound. In 1877, he made a metal disc that moved when sound waves struck it. He attached a needle to the disc, and put the needle's point on a spinning cylinder covered with foil. Sounds made the disc move, which moved the needle. The needle recorded the sounds by marking a pattern on the foil. By running the needle over the marks on the foil, the sound could be heard again. He called his invention the **phonograph**. The first sound ever recorded was Edison saying, "Mary had a little lamb whose fleece was white as snow." The foil cylinder was a long way from a CD, but it made CDs possible.

Edison knew that electricity could be used to make light in a laboratory. He hoped to make light in a form that could be used in homes. For a year, he worked on different ways to do it. In 1879, Edison ran electricity through a piece of burned sewing thread inside a glass bulb. It worked better than anything else he had tried. Edison was not the only inventor working on this problem, but his idea was the most workable. In fact, Edison's first working bulb was not much different from today's light bulbs.

Edison's inventions made him famous. He was known as "The Wizard of Menlo Park." In 1886, he built a much larger laboratory in West Orange, New Jersey. At West Orange, he wanted to invent a machine that "does for the eye what the phonograph does for the ear." In other words, he wanted to invent a device to record moving pictures. Edison knew that if still pictures of a running horse were shown quickly, one after another, it would look as if the horse was moving. After years of experiments, Edison put the still pictures on a long roll of film. He named his invention the **kinetoscope**. After that, Edison and other inventors improved the moving picture machine. Until the 1920s, New Jersey was the movie capital of the world. Fort Lee, New Jersey, was the first "Hollywood."

For the rest of his life, Edison worked to improve the kinetoscope and phonograph. He also made other inventions. When he died in West Orange in 1931, the people of the United States gave him an unusual honor. On the night of his funeral, people all over the country dimmed the lights in their homes and businesses for a few minutes. The dim light honored the man who brought electric light, recorded sound, and moving pictures to the world. ❖❖

Some of Thomas Edison's Inventions		
Invention	**Date**	**What It Did**
improved stock ticker	1869	reported stock market prices
quadruplex	1874	made telegraph carry more messages
telephone transmitter	1877	made voices louder and clearer on telephone
phonograph	1877	recorded sound on foil
light bulb	1879	brought electric light to homes and businesses
kinetoscope	1888–1893	recorded moving pictures
iron ore processor	late 1880s–early 1890s	improved steel production
improved batteries	late 1880s–early 1890s	made longer-lasting storage of electricity for trains and cars
poured concrete house	early 1900s	made stronger foundations for houses
Ediphone	1910s	recording machine for office secretary use

Sample Resources Questions

Directions: Answer the following questions. Base your answer on the article "The Wizard of Menlo Park."

1. Where would you most likely find this passage?
   - Ⓐ in an atlas
   - Ⓑ an almanac
   - Ⓒ in a magazine
   - Ⓓ in the dictionary

2. If you wanted to learn about other famous inventors, which book should you choose?
   - Ⓐ *The Menlo Park Miracle*
   - Ⓑ *Sound and How to Record It*
   - Ⓒ *Thomas Edison: A Biography*
   - Ⓓ *Making Things Work: The History of Inventions*

3. If you wanted to know where Menlo Park is, which resource would be best to use?
   - Ⓐ an atlas
   - Ⓑ a magazine
   - Ⓒ an almanac
   - Ⓓ a newspaper

4. According to the table, when did Edison invent his iron ore processor?
   - Ⓐ after the Edigraph was invented
   - Ⓑ before the phonograph was invented
   - Ⓒ at the same time he invented the quadruplex
   - Ⓓ at the same time he invented his improved batteries

5. According to the table, which invention was used for recording by office secretaries?
   - Ⓐ quadruplex
   - Ⓑ Ediphone
   - Ⓒ kinetoscope
   - Ⓓ phonograph

Additional Practice Questions

Directions: Now try answering some other types of questions about the article. You can learn more about these question types in other lessons of this book.

6. What was the first sound ever recorded?
   - (A) Edison reciting the alphabet
   - (B) birds singing outside Edison's laboratory
   - (C) Edison reciting "Mary Had a Little Lamb"
   - (D) a speech by the President of the United States

7. Which of these statements from the passage is an OPINION?
   - (A) "You should thank Thomas Edison."
   - (B) "He called his invention the phonograph."
   - (C) "He was known as 'The Wizard of Menlo Park.'"
   - (D) "Fort Lee, New Jersey, was the first 'Hollywood.'"

8. Which invention came FIRST?
   - (A) light bulb
   - (B) stock ticker
   - (C) phonograph
   - (D) kinetoscope

9. What is the most likely reason the author wrote this passage?
   - (A) to explain where CDs came from
   - (B) to teach people to become inventors
   - (C) to persuade people to dim their lights
   - (D) to tell about the work of a famous inventor

Lesson 13

Following Directions

Everything seemed to be going perfectly until the explosion.

"What on earth happened?" Ginny asked as she stood staring at the green liquid dripping from the ceiling.

"Uh, I'm not sure." Becky said. She also had heard the loud boom, followed by the sound of something metal hitting the ceiling and crashing to the floor. Both girls had raced into the kitchen to see what all the noise was about. Now they stood looking over the damage: a hole in the ceiling and bits of plaster all over the floor, shreds of green cloth scattered among the wreckage, and green steamy stuff everywhere.

Ginny could tell from the look on her younger sister's face that she knew more than she was letting on. "Okay, Becky. Out with it. What's going on here?"

"Well, I was tie-dying a T-shirt. My friend Jason told me how. I put the dye in the water, and I dropped the shirt in. Then I decided to heat the water so that maybe the colors would come out brighter."

"Is this what you heated the water in?" Ginny pointed at the large pot on the stove.

"Yeah. It was the biggest pot I could find." Becky looked as if she didn't really want to hear what Ginny had to say next.

"Becky, this is Grandma's old pressure cooker. If you don't put the lid on correctly, the top can blow off. If you had been standing over it, you could have been killed."

"Good thing I had to go to the bathroom!" Becky smiled, hoping to get a laugh from her sister. It wasn't working.

"And besides, tie-dyeing is done with cold water, not hot. Didn't you read the directions?"

"What directions?"

"The ones on the box of dye."

"Oh, those. Yeah, I read them . . . sort of. . . . Okay, so I just skimmed the directions. And that was yesterday, just after I bought the dye. Today, I just followed them from memory." Becky looked down at the mess on the floor, then up at the mess everyplace else. "Sort of."

"Good job," Ginny said, peeling a piece of green T-shirt off the kitchen wall. ❖❖

Recipes, video game instructions, directions to a do-it-yourself chemistry set—these are just a few examples of directions you may already use. In this lesson, you will practice following directions closely and carefully.

 ### Read the directions through carefully before you begin.

The easiest way to follow directions is to first get the "big picture." This is like finding the main idea in longer reading passages.

Read all the way through the directions once before you begin working through the steps. Don't just jump in and start mixing ingredients or, worse yet, chemicals. You might run into some not-so-nice surprises in the middle of your project. Also, make sure you understand each step *before* you begin.

 ### Gather all the materials or ingredients you will need.

Before you begin, make sure you have all the necessary items. Gather them in a place close to where you will be working.

 ### Follow the steps in order.

This may seem obvious, but we thought we would mention it anyway. Following directions out of order can bring unwanted results. Also, complete only one step at a time.

Tip 4 **Pay close attention to illustrations.**

Authors often provide pictures, diagrams, or other illustrations along with a passage. Look closely at the illustrations. They are as important as the passage. They will make the passage easier to understand. They may also give extra information that is not in the passage.

Practice Passage

Directions: Read the article "Making Your Own Piñata." Then answer the questions that follow.

Making Your Own Piñata

by Carmilla Schmidt

A piñata (peen-YAH-tah) is a colorful, hollow figure made of papier-mâché or clay. It is often made to look like an animal, such as a bird, fish, cat, or burro. A piñata is filled with candy, toys, and other treats and is used at parties and festivals. The piñata is hung from a tree or ceiling by ropes, which can be used to bounce it up and down. Children, who are blindfolded, try to break the piñata with a stick. They take turns blindly swinging at the moving figure. When the piñata breaks open, they share the treats that fall to the ground.

Piñatas were first made in Spain and have been popular with children in Mexico and the United States for many years. Good piñata makers are often famous in their hometowns. Some piñata makers know how to make hundreds of different animals and shapes.

You don't have to be an expert to make a piñata. You can make your own from papier-mâché. Although it takes time and patience, making your own piñata can be a lot of fun.

What you need:
- assorted balloons
- 1 cup of water
- a large bowl
- cardboard
- masking tape
- paints and brushes or colored tissue paper
- party treats (to fill the piñata)
- 2 cups of flour
- 1 cup of liquid starch
- newspapers
- paper cups

What you do:

If you plan to make a piñata for a party, give yourself plenty of time. It can take several days to make a piñata.

1. Choose a balloon that has the closest shape to the animal you want to make (round, oval, long, skinny, and so on). Blow up the balloon and knot it.

2. Spread newspapers over your work area. Then cut or tear more newspaper in strips about one inch wide.

3. Make a paste by mixing 2 cups of flour, 1 cup of water, and 1 cup of liquid starch in a large bowl. Pull the strips of newspaper through the paste. Squeeze off excess paste by pulling the strips through two fingers. Wrap the papier-mâché strips around the balloon. Leave an opening near the knot so you can put treats in later. Apply three layers of strips, then let the ball dry overnight.

4. After the papier-mâché hardens, pop the balloon, remove it, and throw it away. Use cardboard and paper cups to make legs, ears, or wings. You can make a head by covering a small balloon with strips. Use masking tape to put the parts of your animal together. Then cover the whole body with more papier-mâché.

5. Use paints or colored tissue paper to decorate your piñata. When you are finished, fill it with treats. Then, let the fun begin! ❖❖

Sample Following Directions Questions

Directions: Answer the following questions. Base your answers on the article "Making Your Own Piñata."

1. When making a piñata, which of these should you do LAST?
   Ⓐ Tape the parts of your animal together.
   Ⓑ Cover a balloon with strips of papier-mâché.
   Ⓒ Make legs, wings, or other parts out of cardboard.
   Ⓓ Use paint or tissue paper to decorate your piñata.

2. When should you pop the balloon?
   - Ⓐ just before you put in the treats
   - Ⓑ while you are mixing your paste
   - Ⓒ after the papier-mâché body is all dry
   - Ⓓ as soon as you finish wrapping it with newspaper

3. How is the piñata in Step 5 DIFFERENT from the piñata in Step 4?
   - Ⓐ The piñata in Step 5 is colorful.
   - Ⓑ The piñata in Step 5 does not have treats.
   - Ⓒ The piñata in Step 5 has a balloon inside it.
   - Ⓓ The piñata in Step 5 is covered with papier-mâché.

4. You would like to make a piñata for a party that is one month away. How soon should you start working on your piñata?
   - Ⓐ the day before the party
   - Ⓑ a few hours before the party
   - Ⓒ several days before the party
   - Ⓓ at least one month before the party

Additional Practice Questions

Directions: Now try answering some other types of questions about the article. You'll learn more about these question types in other lessons of this book.

5. This passage might be found in what type of book?
   - Ⓐ drama
   - Ⓑ poetry
   - Ⓒ fiction
   - Ⓓ nonfiction

6. If you wanted to learn more facts about life in Mexico, which of the following books would be the BEST choice?
   - Ⓐ *Popular Mexican Plays*
   - Ⓑ *Mexican Americans Today*
   - Ⓒ *Mexico: Its People and Customs*
   - Ⓓ *Stories and Verses from Mexico*

7. Which of the following statements from the article is an OPINION?

    Ⓐ   "A piñata is filled with candy, toys, and other treats . . ."

    Ⓑ   "Piñatas were first made in Spain . . ."

    Ⓒ   "You can make your own from papier-mâché."

    Ⓓ   ". . . making your own piñata can be a lot of fun."

8. Why did the author write this article?

    Ⓐ   to teach people how a piñata is made

    Ⓑ   to persuade people to travel to Mexico

    Ⓒ   to persuade people to try Spanish foods

    Ⓓ   to tell about famous Spanish artists

9. Why do you think piñatas are so popular? Use details and information from the article in your answer.

_____

_____

_____

_____

_____

_____

_____

_____

Lesson 14

What's It to Ya?

Reading is most fun when we connect the things we read to our own lives. Stories and articles may remind you of things that have happened to you before. They also may make you think through your own opinions about an issue.

Practice Passage

Directions: Read the story "It Could Be Worse." It will help you understand the lesson.

It Could Be Worse

by Marie Render

"This is the most embarrassing thing that's ever happened to me!" Maureen said. She was looking at herself in the bathroom mirror. Traces of ketchup clung to her bangs and eyebrows. Her eyes, bloodshot from crying, nearly matched the red streaks on her white shirt. "I look like I'm starring in a bad horror movie," she moaned.

"Oh, come on, Maureen," said Kelsie. "I already said I was sorry. Besides, I couldn't help it. The ketchup wouldn't come out of the bottle. When I squeezed it, the whole mess just shot out at you." Kelsie wrung out another wet paper towel and handed it to her friend. She already felt bad enough without having Maureen remind her.

"Try to look on the bright side, Maureen. Worse things have happened to you before."

"Oh, yeah? Like what?" Maureen scrubbed furiously at a long red streak on her blouse. It looked like an arrow pointing from her chin to her belly button. The harder she rubbed, the wider it got. "What could be worse than getting blasted with ketchup in front of everybody in the lunchroom?"

"Remember the time you ripped your pants on the jungle gym in kindergarten?" Kelsie said. "You didn't even know they were ripped until Tracy Swanson started telling everybody your underwear was showing."

"Ughhhh. Don't remind me. I had to wait in the nurse's office until my mom brought me another pair of jeans. I thought I would *die* of embarrassment."

"Yeah, but you didn't. And almost everybody forgot about it by the next Monday," Kelsie said.

"Everybody but Tracy," Maureen said. "She never stopped reminding me about it until she moved away at the end of first grade." Most of the ketchup was out of Maureen's blouse by now. It didn't look as good as it had before lunch, but at least it looked better than it had a few minutes ago.

"And don't forget about the time you ended up flat on your face in front of Ja-cob Mar-tin!" Kelsie said. She giggled, remembering how Maureen had gotten so nervous when the new boy said "Hi" to her that she tripped and fell in front of him.

"Thanks for reminding me," Maureen groaned. She pressed the button on the hand drier and aimed the nozzle at her wet blouse.

"And what about the time in third grade when you laughed so hard at the movies that you wet your pants?" Kelsie asked.

"Do you write all these things down, Kelsie? I'll bet you have a notebook called *Maureen's Most Embarrassing Moments*."

"Hey, that's an idea!" Kelsie said. "Let's write a book about all the things that have happened to you and send it to Oprah. I'm sure she'll call us up and ask us to be on TV. Then someday you can tell your grandchildren about the time you tripped and fell on top of a famous TV star—in front of millions of people! Now that would be really embarrassing!"

Maureen laughed. "Okay, Kelsie," she said. "You've made your point. I guess a little ketchup shower isn't the worst thing that could happen. But I can't help wishing it had happened to somebody else." She looked at her friend's clean T-shirt and grinned. "Let's get back to lunch. I think I need to put some ketchup on my fries." ❖❖

Personal Response Tips

Here are a few tips for writing a personal response to a reading passage.

 Read the question carefully.

Make sure you understand the question being asked. Personal response questions can be asked in many ways. Three examples follow.

Sample Question 1
Think of a time when you felt embarrassed. How was your embarrassing time similar to or different from Maureen's? Use details from the story to explain your answer.

Sample Question 2

Have you ever caused an accident that embarrassed someone else or caused them trouble? Compare the way you handled the problem with the way Kelsie does in the story.

Sample Question 3

What do you think is the best way to handle an embarrassing moment? Do you agree with the way Maureen and Kelsie deal with embarrassment in the story? Or do you have another idea for handling embarrassment? Use details from the story to explain your answer.

 Support your response with details from the passage.

It is important that you give specific reasons for your answer. Use as many specific details and examples from the passage as you can, but write them in your own words.

1. Look at the questions under Tip 1. Choose one sample question and answer it on the lines below. Base your answer on the story "It Could Be Worse."

_____

_____

_____

_____

_____

_____

_____

_____

_____

_____

_____

_____

_____

_____

_____

_____

_____

_____

 Answer all parts of the question.

Be very thorough in answering personal response questions. Some of these questions may have more than one part. Be sure to answer each part of the question.

 Use your best handwriting.

You don't need to worry about spelling or grammar. But you do need to make sure that others can read what you have written. Use your best handwriting. If you need to make changes in your work, erase or cross out as neatly as you can.

Tip 5 **Express your own opinion.**

You might agree or disagree with the ideas in a story or article. A personal response question is asking for *your* ideas about the passage. Don't be afraid to say what you really think. (But remember to use details and examples from the passage to support your answer.)

Practice Passage

Directions: Read the article "Come to Alaska." Then answer the questions that follow.

Come to Alaska

Many people think of Alaska as only snowy, icy wilderness—the land of igloos and sled-dog races. To the half-million people who live here and the countless others who visit each year, Alaska is much, much more.

Separated from the "lower 48" states by almost 500 miles of Canadian territory, Alaska is perfect for a real <u>getaway</u>. Visit our bustling cities and historic coastal towns, where you can enjoy our many museums, theaters, and restaurants. Numerous festivals are held across the state throughout the year. And don't pass up our smaller villages, such as Saxman, home of the world's largest collection of authentic totem poles.

Settlers came seeking their fortunes in furs in the 1700s, gold in the 1800s, and oil during this century. We believe that future generations will come in search of Alaska's most abundant treasure—its landscape. Alaska is the largest state in the Union, more than twice the size of Texas. Much of it is still undisturbed by humans—rolling hills, sparkling lakes, majestic glaciers, swampy river valleys, and big-sky plains. Forests cover almost a third of the state. Alaska boasts the 16 highest mountain peaks in North America, along with several active volcanoes. Whether it is snowskiing, kayaking, fishing, or hiking, you'll find it all here.

Alaska's climate is as varied as its landscape. Warm winds that blow in from the ocean create a mild climate in the southern regions. During the summer, the sun shines about 20 hours a day. Average precipitation (rain, snow, and sleet) is about 55 inches per year. Average temperatures across the state range between –11° F in the winter to 59° F in the summer.

Come to Alaska. You'll find out why it is one of the fastest growing states in the country. And maybe you'll decide to stay.

Sample Personal Response Question

Directions: Answer the following question. Base your answer on the article "Come to Alaska."

1. Would you like to live in Alaska? What might be enjoyable about living there? What might be unpleasant? Use details from the article to support your answer.

_____

_____

_____

_____

_____

_____

_____

_____

_____

_____

_____

Additional Practice Questions

Directions: Now try answering some other types of questions about the article. You can learn more about these question types in other lessons of this book.

2. What does *getaway* mean?
   - Ⓐ festival
   - Ⓑ vacation
   - Ⓒ landscape
   - Ⓓ wilderness

3. Why did the author write this article?
   - Ⓐ to persuade people to visit Alaska
   - Ⓑ to compare Alaska to other states
   - Ⓒ to tell people about the history of Alaska
   - Ⓓ to persuade people to learn about winter sports

4. Which of the following is a statement of FACT?
   - Ⓐ "Many people think of Alaska as only snowy, icy wilderness—the land of igloos and sled-dog races."
   - Ⓑ "To the half-million people who live here . . . Alaska is much, much more."
   - Ⓒ "We believe that future generations will come in search of Alaska's most abundant treasure—its landscape."
   - Ⓓ "Alaska is the largest state in the Union, more than twice the size of Texas."

5. Which of the following is a statement of OPINION?
   - Ⓐ "Settlers came seeking their fortunes in furs in the 1700s, . . ."
   - Ⓑ "During the summer, the sun shines about 20 hours a day."
   - Ⓒ "Average precipitation is about 55 inches per year."
   - Ⓓ "You'll find out why it is one of the fastest growing states in the country."

APPENDIX – To the Teacher

Blast Off on New Jersey Reading addresses the objectives listed below and on the following page.

New Jersey Elementary School Proficiency Assessment (ESPA) Objectives

Reading

Students construct and extend meaning through reading.

A. A student should know:	*Blast Off* Lesson
• That reading is a way of thinking, learning, and communicating.	all lessons
• That speaking, viewing, listening, and writing contribute to reading.	4, 12, 13
• Strategies to read a variety of texts.	4
• Literary forms (e.g., plays, poetry, short stories), elements (e.g., alliteration, metaphor), and devices (e.g., foreshadowing, flashback).	11, 12
• That authors and readers have purposes.	10
• That critical thinking, reflection, and analysis contribute to the reading experience.	all lessons
• That reflection on multiple perspectives and texts helps the reader construct meaning.	10
B. A student should be able to:	*Blast Off* Lesson
• Use and adjust reading strategies to construct (comprehend) meaning.	4
• Collaborate with others to develop meanings of texts.	4

• Make connections between:
  – the text and self
  – the text and others
  – the text and other texts
	4, 10, 12

• Interpret literary forms (e.g., short stories, poetry, dramas, novels, essays), elements, and devices.	11, 12
• Draw on experience for reading.	4

Language Arts and Literacy Standards and Progress Indicators

Cumulative Progress Indicators

Standard 3.4: All students will read various materials and texts with comprehension and critical analysis.

By the end of Grade 4, students:	*Blast Off* Lesson
1. Use listening, speaking, writing, and viewing to assist with reading.	4, 12, 13
2. Listen and respond to whole texts.	14
3. Understand that authors write for different purposes, such as persuading, informing, entertaining, and instructing.	10
4. Use reading for different purposes, such as enjoyment, learning, and problem-solving.	12
5. Read independently a variety of literature written by authors of different cultures, ethnicities, genders, and ages.	all lessons
6. Read literally, inferentially, and critically.	1, 2, 3, 7, 8, 9
7. Use print concepts in developmentally appropriate ways.	all lessons
8. Read with comprehension.	all lessons
9. Use prior knowledge to extend reading ability and comprehension and to link aspects of the text with experiences and people in their own lives.	4, 14
10. Identify passages in the text that support their point of view.	10, 14
11. Distinguish personal opinions and points of view from those of the author, and distinguish fact from opinion.	10, 14
12. Demonstrate comprehension through retelling or summarizing ideas and following written directions.	4, 13
13. Identify elements of a story, such as characters, setting, and sequence of events.	2, 5, 6
14. Identify literary forms, such as fiction, poetry, drama, and nonfiction.	12
15. Expand vocabulary using appropriate strategies and techniques such as word analysis and context clues.	3
16. Read and use printed materials and technical manuals from other disciplines, such as science, social studies, mathematics, and applied technology.	12